AF269667

With shimmering golden sands, pine-scented mountains,
2,000-year-old labyrinthine streets and dazzling Modernista
architecture, Barcelona is a whirlwind romance of a city,
an irresistible temptress that seduces at every turn. From people-
watching and tapas bar-hopping through the old fisherman's quarter
to exploring museums, ateliers and indie stores of the old town, this
Catalan city thrills and inspires in equal measure.

For some, it's an escape to wild fiestas and balmy nights of
debauchery. For others, it's a much needed dose of art and culture,
an epicurean dream. And while many jet in with the intention of
staying only for a year or so, Barcelona teems with those who were
won over by the city's charms and made their move a permanent one.

Big enough to get lost in, but small enough to explore in a weekend,
all you need is a little insider knowledge and an adventurous spirit to
get a feel for what it is about this intoxicating, illustrious place that
enchants everyone who visits. Some say you can't have it all.
Bring them to Barcelona, I say.

the hunt barcelona writer

ben holbrook

Born and raised in South Wales' Gower Peninsula, Ben Holbrook spent
much of his youth exploring the world with his travel agent parents.
His first job was stacking brochures in his mother's office, which may
explain why he ended up becoming a travel writer himself. Ben moved
to Barcelona in 2009, and when he isn't writing about his adoptive
home city on his blog, driftwoodjournals.com, he can be found hunting
out new cultural and culinary experiences around the world, writing
for various international publications and indulging in his penchant
for good wine and craft beer.

CASA CAMPER

Urban chic in the arts and culture district

Carrer d'Elisabets, 11 (near Carrer del Notariat) / +34 933 426 280 / casacamper.com

Double from €198

For a heavy dose of creative inspiration, the Casa Camper design hotel,
and its prime location in the city's cultural hub of El Raval, is ideal.
Occupying a traditional 19th-century Gothic tenement, Jordi Tió and
Ferran Amat have created atypical spaces that maximize modern urban living.
And with the much lauded restaurant, Dos Palillos, a temple of Iberian-Asian
fusion led by Albert Raurich, a disciple of culinary luminary Ferran Adrià,
it's a tempting choice for discerning gastronauts.

HOTEL BRUMMELL

Respite from the hustle and bustle

Carrer Nou de la Rambla, 174 (near Carrer de Magalhães)
+34 931 258 622 / hotelbrummell.com

Double from €90

An intimate, stylish oasis, Hotel Brummell sits at the foot of the
verdant Montjuïc and achieves informal sophistication with luxurious
bespoke furniture and modern detailing in the sun-drenched rooms.
A modish sundeck and petite pool area set the scene for body bronzing
and wine tasting. The Box Social restaurant's open-air patio is the
perfect spot for exploring new flavors.

HOTEL NERI

Gothic sophistication

Carrer de Sant Sever, 5 (near Carrer de Sant Honorat)
+34 933 040 655 / hotelneri.com

Double from €295

Deep in the heart of the Gothic quarter, within stumbling distance
from the Catedral de Barcelona and the delights of the city center,
Hotel Neri is housed in a 17th-century mansion that epitomizes
Barcelona's old-meets-new aesthetic. Thick stone walls, period features
and modern art combine to create tasteful living spaces, and its leafy
courtyard restaurant and rooftop bar offer gourmet Mediterranean
dining and superlative views over the city.

HOTEL OMM

Trailblazing design

Carrer del Rosselló, 265 (near Passeig de Gràcia)
+34 934 454 000 / hotelomm.com

Double from €224

The first and most lauded of Barcelona's design hotels, Hotel Omm
is the complete package: minimalist yet comfortable rooms, spas,
a rooftop pool and stellar views of the city's most emblematic buildings
– Gaudí's Casa Milà and Sagrada Familia. Its Michelin-starred restaurant,
Roca Moo, is overseen by the team behind El Celler de Can Roca (named
"The Best Restaurant in the World" by *Restaurant* magazine in 2013),
but make sure you book a table well in advance as reservations are
snatched up quickly here.

HOTEL PRAKTIK BAKERY

Sweet sleeps

Carrer de Provença, 279 (near Carrer de Pau Claris) / +34 934 880 061
hotelpraktikbakery.com

Double from €62

There's nothing better than waking up to the smell of fresh bread. Except for the smell wafting to you as you wake up in Eixample. Anna Bellsolà, owner of Baluard Bakery (see pg 116) in Barceloneta, teamed up with Praktik Hotels to create an upscale yet homey urban retreat, which means your breakfast just got a bit sweeter. Don't miss their selection of breads and pastries, baked right inside the hotel. Its prime location mere meters off the glittering, Gaudí-heavy Passeig de Gràcia is an added bonus.

OHLA HOTEL

Contemporary luxury

Via Laietana, 49 (near Carrer de Comtal) / +34 933 415 050 / ohlahotel.com

Double from €196

With its majestic neoclassical façade and modern interiors, 74-room Ohla Hotel stands pride of place on the arterial Via Laietana. Originally the first Count of Barcelona's city dwelling, this palatial haven draws in scenesters with its bars for tapas and cocktails, an outdoor "chill-out lounge" and the Michelin-starred Saüc restaurant. But for guests, it's the awe-inspiring city views from the rooftop terrace and swimming pool that steal the show.

THE5ROOMS

Home away from home

Carrer de Pau Claris, 72 (near Plaça d'Urquinaona)
+34 933 427 880 / the5rooms.com

Double from €127

If you want to feel what it's like to actually live in Barcelona, The5rooms presents a fantastic opportunity. Owner Yessica Delgado has created a warm and inviting ambiance by drawing on natural materials, like exposed brick, and the building's ornate design heritage to create rooms and apartments that are effortlessly stylish and livable.

el raval

A kaleidoscope of different ethnicities on the southwest side of La Rambla (or Les Rambles, as it's called in Catalan), El Raval is Barcelona's most dynamic and exciting neighborhood. Cheap rents and creative thinkers have transformed it from an old, crime-ridden part of the city into an arts-driven hub of counterculture, where bohemians mix with solopreneurs and professional skateboarders. Roam the bustling streets and you'll find a remarkable array of independent shops selling tempting trinkets, or kick back on one of the leaf-shaded boulevards where you can sip on cocktails and indulge in international cuisine. It's also home to many of Barcelona's most important cultural institutions, housing an abundance of museums and galleries, including the city's oldest religious site, Sant Pau del Camp. True, it's a little rough around the edges, but El Raval is not a place you want to miss.

1 Bun Bo Viêtnam
2 Dtox Hair Salon
3 Fantastik
4 Fatbottom Llibreria Gràfica
5 Filmoteca de Catalunya
6 Flax & Kale
7 Grey Street
8 Grube Guitars
9 Lullaby Vintage Store
10 Museu d'Art Contemporari de Barcelona
11 Sant Pau del Camp

BUN BO VIÊTNAM

Southeast Asian flavor in BCN

Carrer dels Àngels, 6 (near Carrer del Carme) / +34 934 121 890
bunboraval.com / Open daily

Just a short stroll away from the national library and a university, it's no surprise that this tree-and-restaurant-lined street is teeming with well-heeled students and bushy-tailed bohemians. It's also home to Bun Bo Viêtnam, a suitably youthful and vibrant restaurant illuminated by electric pink and yellow lanterns and glittering shrines to Quan Am, the bodhisattva of mercy. Traditional dishes such as pho and bok choy sautéed with garlic will satisfy even the most venerable of Vietnamese cuisine devotees, while the crispy spring rolls and prawn-filled wontons are perfect for tapas-style sharing. To wash everything down, I'm fond of the extra-dry Asahi beer, and the house mojitos are the stuff of legend. Don't leave without trying the mango ice cream and Vietnamese coffee.

DTOX HAIR SALON

Tresses to impress

Carrer dels Tallers, 77 (near Carrer de Valldonzella) / +34 931 246 091
dtoxbcn.com / Closed Sunday and Monday

Though I've since learned the language, I could write a book about the hilarious, and often heartbreaking, experiences I had as a verbally illiterate newbie in Barcelona. Most of it would be set in some random backstreet barber shop. After numerous styling disasters, I gave up on the idea of cutting my hair altogether, opting instead to let it grow long and wild. Eventually I tried cutting it myself, but that didn't go too well. Thankfully, I found Dtox Hair Salon, a sanctuary of personal transformation, where the stylists are more than just English speakers: these are the people styling the locks of the city's most hip. With owners Carolina Suasi and Jesús Prados on your side, you'll never have to live with a badly translated haircut ever again.

FANTASTIK

Rare items from across the globe

Carrer de Joaquín Costa, 62 (near Passatge de Sant Bernat)
+34 933 013 068 / **fantastik.es** / **Closed Sunday**

To me, Barcelona feels like some kind of Promised Land for idealists, a place where even the zaniest dreamers can make a living doing what they love: for example, the famous donut hawker who balances his stock on his head as he dances up and down the beach; the Spanish Bob Dylan busker; and the owners of many offbeat stores, such as this one. This global bazaar stocks hundreds of colorful curiosities sourced from developing countries all over the world. Treat yourself to quirky kitchenware from Mexico, handmade jewelry from Cambodia, bicycle accessories from India, clockwork toys from China or even a plastic pink flamingo. All said, this is one magnificent celebration of internationally made items.

FATBOTTOM LLIBRERIA GRÀFICA

Comics, illustrated novels and more

Carrer de la Lluna, 10 (near Carrer de Cardona) / +34 931 798 957
fatbottombooks.com / Closed Sunday

They call comic book fanatics "los freakies" in Spain, but the term has a different connotation to its English translation. I mean, if you're a "freaky", you're still considered strange, but the difference is that, here, it's not purely a designation for deviants. In fact, it's considered kind of cool. I imagine it has something to do with the city's annual comic convention, which draws said freakies from far and wide. Then there are the stunning illustrated bookstores like Fatbottom Llibreria Gràfica. It's an Aladdin's cave of graphic novels, children's books, classic comics and traditional artistic illustrations. They also specialize in books and prints from Spanish artists, self-published comics and small-print fanzines. Swing by and pick up something that strikes your fancy. You can be freaky, too.

FILMOTECA DE CATALUNYA

A movie buff's dream

Plaça de Salvador Seguí, 1 (near Carrer de Sant Pau)
+34 935 671 070 / **filmoteca.cat** / **Open daily**

When a friend asked if I would like to go and see an art house movie in El Raval, I imagined some kind of derelict building with damp sofas and stale popcorn. When I arrived at Filmoteca de Catalunya, I was astonished to find that it was a vast, cinematic temple with two screens, complete with exhibition rooms and a library. The objective here is to recover, preserve and promote film culture, regardless of style, origin or category, as well as camera and audio equipment. Programs tend to follow a set theme: one week might be dedicated to the work of Tim Burton, the next to Shakespeare. If you don't have time for a movie, I suggest just checking out the exhibition room, which is free to enter.

FLAX & KALE

Healthy bites

Carrer del Tallers, 74 (near Carrer de Gravina) / **+34 933 175 664**
teresacarles.com/fk / **Open daily**

Floor to ceiling windows allow this space to be flooded with natural sunlight, fueling impassioned conversations about clean eating between yoga-toned diners. Flax & Kale is Spain's first flexitarian restaurant, but even though it feels like it's straight out of Los Angeles – with a jet-set crowd to match – it's actually the brainchild of the Feel Good Food Group, which has been leading Barcelona's vegetarian scene since 1979, when Teresa Carles Healthy Foods opened. The menu here promotes healthy eating in a spectacularly fervent way: raw food, gluten-free ingredients and oily fish dominate the menu, with dishes like spelt flatbread with smoked eggplant and sardines, and salmon sashimi toast. Go for the famous weekend brunch menu if you don't mind waiting for a table, and don't miss the invigorating juices.

GREY STREET

Delightful little gift shop

**Carrer del Peu de la Creu, 25 (near Carrer de la Lluna)
+34 931 743 506 / greystreetbarcelona.com / Closed Sunday**

Grey Street is one of those heartwarming places that instantly make you feel right at home. This mini emporium of wonderful gifts and unique trinkets is the work of Australian owner Amy, who named the store after the street where her grandparents live in Canberra. Her creative approach has led to collaborations with many local artists and designers, as well as international artisans. Curating everything from gorgeously illustrated stationery and Spanish pottery to vintage clothing and handmade jewelry, there's something for everyone here, whether you want a dainty €1 souvenir or you're looking for something extra special for a loved one.

GRUBE GUITARS

Handcrafted instruments

Carrer de Requesens, 7 (near Carrer del Príncep de Viana)
+34 930 046 102 / grubeguitars.com / Closed Saturday and Sunday

Stepping through the wine-red doors, the smell of toasted wood and hot metal filled my senses. A fan blew the ravaging sounds of Led Zeppelin's "Immigrant Song" around the modest space as Sebastien (Mr Grube himself) powered down his tools and looked up at me through his dusty, long hair. His giant hand engulfed mine as I introduced myself and with one quick look at my beloved Stratocaster, he distinguished himself as a master luthier, pinpointing the problems without me saying a word. But he doesn't just revive old guitars; he also crafts his own artisanal pieces, sculpting everything from solid body beauties to semi-hollow howlers. He'll even hand-build one especially for you, if you ask nicely.

LULLABY VINTAGE STORE

High-end retro

Carrer de la Riera Baixa, 22 (near Carrer de Picalquers)
+34 934 430 802 / facebook.com/lullaby-vintage / Closed Sunday

Joan and Africa fell in love – first with fashion, then with each other.
When they both lost their jobs, they decided it was the perfect time to follow
their dream of opening their own boutique. And thank the heavens that
they did, because their shop has made hard-to-find designer wear not only
attainable, but also affordable. They stock both men's and women's fashion,
and a particularly covetable collection of designer handbags and sunglasses
sourced from Paris, Milan and Rome. But it's Joan and Africa's passion for
helping their customers achieve their desired look that makes shopping here
such a joy. Take a deep breath, say hello and let them take care of the rest.

MUSEU D'ART CONTEMPORARI DE BARCELONA

Contemporary art for the daring

**Plaça dels Àngels, 1 (near Carrer de Montalegre) / +34 934 120 810
macba.cat/en / Closed Tuesday**

If you like art galleries where you're gently guided by a docent through serene landscapes and pleasant portraits, this is probably not for you. There's nothing "easy" about this maverick of a museum. In fact, with its evocative, cryptic and outright baffling displays, MACBA errs on the side of inaccessible. However, if you can open and focus your mind for long enough, you'll be rewarded with the beauty of abstract political and cultural art pieces, as well as the 10 temporary exhibitions that pass through the doors each season. There are free children's workshops, lectures and guided tours if you need a little help getting your head around things. Be strong. You can do it.

SANT PAU DEL CAMP

The oldest church in Barcelona

Carrer de Sant Pau, 101 (near Carrer de les Carretes) / +34 934 410 001
webs.ono.com/santpaudelcamp / Closed Sunday

Sant Pau del Camp may not have the snazzy spires of Gaudí's Sagrada Familia or the soaring ceilings of Santa Maria del Mar, but it does have a staggering amount of history: in fact, this Romanesque marvel has over a thousand years of it. The current location, in the thick of El Raval, betrays its name, which translates to "Saint Paul of the countryside". Until the turn of the 14th century, it was surrounded by nothing but fields, fruit orchards, farms and monks. So as you take in the sights of its thick stone walls and modest scale, just mull this over for a moment: this unassuming little church is about 800 years older than America. Eight. Hundred. Years.

caffeine fix

Barcelona's third-wave coffee shops

Upon arriving in Barcelona in 2009, I was heavily dependent on regular caffeine hits to function. To my dismay, I found little repose among generic UHT-infused cups of café con leche. Thankfully, the city has slowly filled with independent coffee shops that are roasting their own beans, brewing their own blends and handcrafting cups of liquid inspiration so good that my veins pump freely and wildly once again.

Nømad Coffee Lab & Shop was the first local company to start actively educating the population about the joys of quality beans and is where the most enlightened caffeine-enthusiasts can be found. But I must forewarn you that, as owner Jordi Mestre says himself, this is "a place for tasting coffee", not for whiling away an afternoon.

Federal Café and its Australian owners bring with them a double shot of coffee mastery. Famed for transforming Sant Antoni's Parlament Street into a hipster haven, this is also where brunch became "a thing" in Barcelona. For those only interested in the black stuff, I suggest skipping the rowdy brunch rush and turning up a bit later to take it easy on the shaded rooftop terrace.

Satan's Coffee Corner is an urban-inspired joint complete with thumping hip-hop and open-fronted barista stations. Marco and his team offer the works – cold brews, pour-overs and filter coffees – although, as a traditionalist myself, I have to recommend their perfectly balanced espresso, a shot of which comes with crema so thick you'll be scooping it up with a spoon.

If you're the type who likes to eat with your coffee, you won't want to miss **Caravelle**. Owned and operated by Australian-British couple Zim and Poppy, not only do they grind Nømad's beans to perfection, they also make every element of the American-European menu in-house to create dishes such as the impeccable Cuban sandwich, made with slow-roasted pork and handmade pickles. Plus, they have house-brand craft beers. This is my kind of coffee shop.

CARAVELLE
Carrer del Pintor Fortuny, 31 (near Carrer del Doctor Dou), +34 933 179 892, caravelle.es, open daily

FEDERAL CAFÉ
Carrer del Parlament, 39 (near Carrer del Comte Borrell), +34 931 873 607, federalcafe.es
closed Monday

NØMAD COFFEE LAB & SHOP
Passatge Sert, 12 (near Carrer de Sant Pere Més Alt)
+34 628 566 235, nomadcoffee.es
closed Saturday and Sunday

SATAN'S COFFEE CORNER
Carrer de l'Arc de Sant Ramon del Call, 11
(near Placeta de Manuel Ribé), +34 666 222 599
satanscoffee.com, open daily

el barri gòtic

The Gothic Quarter, or El Barri Gòtic in Catalan, is the oldest neighborhood in Barcelona and continues to be the city's physical and cultural heart. Its history dates back to the Roman Empire, when it was a walled city called Barcino. You can still see the remains of the 2,000-year-old defense walls and medieval buildings, as well as a splendid array of romantic plaças, Baroque churches and Gothic cathedrals. Stretching from the northeast side of La Rambla to Via Laietana, its winding streets – crammed with all sorts of little indie shops and artisanal workshops, as well as countless bohemian cafés, bars and restaurants serving everything from traditional Catalan fare to life-changing haute cuisine – are perfect for exploring on foot. Put the map away and allow yourself to get lost. You won't regret it.

1 Bar Mariatchi
2 Barcelona Street Style Tour
3 Caelum
4 Café de l'Académia
5 Čaj Chai Teashop
6 Cook&Taste
7 El Changuito
8 Formatgeria La Seu
9 Harlem Jazz Club
10 Home on Earth
11 Kælderkold
12 La Cerería
13 Sor Rita Bar (off map)
14 Zoen

BAR MARIATCHI

Backstreet drinks and tunes

Carrer dels Còdols, 14 (near Carrer d'En Rull) / No phone
mariatchi.com / Open daily

Walking down a dark street in the heart of the Gothic quarter one night,
I was instructed by friends to stay close to the wall and not look up, as those
who live near this bar have been known to announce their displeasure when
the bar gets too noisy by, ahem, pouring water on passersby. As if on cue,
an angry tirade rang out from a balcony above us, followed by the sound of
water thundering onto the street. Inside Bar Mariatchi, the walls are painted
in random blocks of color, and the "furniture" consists of plastic chairs and
empty beer kegs for tables. The crowd is capricious yet benevolent, with a
wild mix of bohemian types and musicians who meet to jam into the early
hours (hence the water). Sip on the bar's infamous house cocktails and let
the good times roll. If you get soaked, at least it's a good story!

BARCELONA STREET STYLE TOUR

I spy with my little eye...

Meeting point: Plaça George Orwell (near Carrer del Escudellers)
No phone / barcelonastreetstyletour.com / Open daily

I doubt there's a single street in Barcelona that hasn't been jazzed up with a touch of street art splendor. Not that all of it can be classed as progressive, or even good, mind you, but if you know the right places, you'll soon see why Barcelona is so often heralded as one of the world's leading street art cities. That's where Barcelona Street Style Tour comes in. Their three-hour bike tour starts in El Barri Gòtic and heads through the 22@Barcelona district in El Poblenou, taking you directly to where the remains of the industrial revolution are brought back to life with inspirational graffiti pieces, paste-ups and large scale murals. Trust me on this: even if you're not into street art, this tour is a fantastic way to learn about some of Barcelona's most colorful neighborhoods.

CAELUM

Nun-made treats

**Carrer de la Palla, 8 (near Carrer del Banys Nous) / +34 933 026 993
caelumbarcelona.com / Open daily**

I might not go to church on Sundays, but I do make a weekly pilgrimage
to Caelum. As a Brit, I revel in the chintzy décor and the excellent selection
of teas. It's the handcrafted treats, however, that really stir the soul, with
such timeless classics as cinnamon-spiced cakes, almond puff pastries
and Seville cider cakes, all handmade by nuns in monasteries across Spain.
There are plenty of savory temptations to tickle your fancy, too. You can
also sip on Trappist beers and various other monk-made brews, though
it's the treacle-thick hot chocolate that'll really put hairs on your chest.
There's literally nowhere else like it in the city, so put on your Sunday
best and come on down.

CAFÉ DE L'ACADÉMIA

Delicious Catalan cuisine in a lovely setting

**Carrer dels Lledó, 1 (near Carrer del Bisbe Caçador) / +34 933 198 253
No website / Closed Saturday and Sunday**

No trip to Barcelona would be complete without an al fresco lunch with inspiring views. Instead of settling at a place on La Rambla, follow the trickling sounds of the medieval water fountain and looming church bell towers to the transcendant square of Plaça de Sant Just, which dates back to the 14th century. Enjoying one of Barcelona's most privileged settings, Café de l'Académia is a modern Catalan restaurant offering traditional regional cuisine, with hearty meat feasts and wondrous Mediterranean seafood. What's more, owner Jordi Casteldi is a vintner, which makes this one a fantastic spot to sample the fruits of the local terroir. Just be sure to keep an afternoon free – this is the long and lazy lunch of your dreams.

ČAJ CHAI TEASHOP

Artisanal teahouse

Carrer de Sant Domenec del Call, 12 (near Carrer de la Fruita)
+34 933 019 592 / cajchai.com / Open daily

Much as I love this city and its insatiable lust for life, there are times when it all gets a bit much, especially during the summer rush. When I find myself adrift in my own skin, suffering from inevitable bouts of sensory overload, I take myself to the tonic that is Čaj Chai Teashop. Spanish-American owner Antonio has a serenity about him as he delicately picks and prepares teas from his 140-strong stock. The dark pu-erh teas, which Antonio describes as being "both bitter and sweet at the same time", are my picks, but there are also yellow, white, green and Himalayan teas, as well as chai and herbal brews. What's more, you can purchase tea and Japanese or Korean teapots to enjoy in your own home.

COOK&TASTE

Half-day cooking classes

Carrer del Paradís, 3 (near Carrer de la Pietat) / **+34 933 021 320**
cookandtaste.net / **Open daily**

My happiest childhood memories are of my mother teaching me
how to cook her legendary lasagne. Something else she taught me is
that to understand a new culture, you have to understand its cuisine.
While Barcelona's outstanding array of restaurants and tapas bars will do
a pretty darn good job of getting you up to speed, if you want to dig a little
deeper, dive into the kitchen at Cook&Taste. Their hands-on classes and
knowledgeable staff will reveal the secrets of perfecting authentic Spanish
cuisine, with everything from Catalan mountain fare to classic paella and
sensational Mediterranean seafood dishes. And the icing on the cake: classes
start with a tour of the Boqueria food market. My mother would love it here.

EL CHANGUITO

Restored antiques and art

Passatge de la Pau, 13 (near Carrer de Josep Anselm Clavé)
+34 933 106 326 / elchanguito.com / Closed Sunday and Monday

Ever since my grandfather bestowed his beloved pocket watch to me, I have been fanatical about antiques and the storied lives they have lived before mine even began. Luckily, Barcelona is quite the destination for tenacious treasure hunters. Passionate travelers and collectors, the owners of El Changuito have dedicated their lives to finding and restoring the forgotten riches of bygone times. From furniture to glassware, jewelry to artwork, they stock the lot. Often unable to let them go, the nicest pieces are kept in their own home, until, that is, they need to free up space for their latest finds and are forced to sell. Don't feel bad for them though. Ultimately, their loss is your gain.

FORMATGERIA LA SEU

Stellar Spanish cheeses

**Carrer de la Dageuria, 16 (near Carrer del Bisbe Caçador)
+34 934 126 548 / formatgerialaseu.com / Closed Sunday and Monday**

Since moving to Barcelona, my diet has morphed beyond all recognition. Though I'll never renounce my tea and toast breakfast ritual, hearty pies and roast dinners have been replaced with a few select staples: bread (oven-warm), olives, cured ham and cheese. This is what I eat as a snack, for lunch and dinner, whether I want to treat myself or even if I need to tighten the purse strings. And believe me, once you've sampled the handcrafted produce of Formatgeria La Seu, you'll want to do the same. The shelves are stocked with the finest cheeses from Spain's rural producers, providing an astounding array of flavors and textures from crumbly and tangy to blue and creamy. For the adventurous epicurean, the seductive goat cheese ice creams are just the ticket.

HARLEM JAZZ CLUB

The oldest concert hall in Barcelona

Carrer de Comtessa de Sobradiel, 8 (near Carrer d'Ataülf)
+34 933 100 755 / harlemjazzclub.es / Open daily

Stroll the streets in the late afternoon and you'll see that the city seems to be teeming with saxophone-toting jazz cats and guitar-wielding blues hounds. Where they spend their days, I can't say, but the nights are a different story. Over the last few decades, Barcelona has quietly become the cradle of Spanish blues and jazz, and although there are countless open mic venues and basement bonanzas, it's Harlem Jazz Club that sits at the crossroads of it all. This venerable venue grinds and grooves with the live sounds of everything from bolero calypso and Cuban clave to rockabilly swing and funk on a nightly basis.

HOME ON EARTH
Sustainable design and fun gifts
Carrer de la Boqueria, 14 (near Carrer d'en Quintana)
+34 933 158 558 / homeonearth.com / Open daily
Just for a moment, try to picture your life as a professional treasure hunter, traveling the world in search of artisan craftsmanship and beautiful products. Well, that is the life of Mette and Stefan, a Danish-German couple who travel the globe looking for nature-inspired pieces to stock their serene retail space. Everything here is handmade using renewable materials and traditional production methods, with a broad array of items ranging from bamboo xylophones to coconut mixing bowls, fossil stone jewelry to hand-carved children's toys. You can even find elegant garden products and high-end bicycles. If it's green, it's here. I can't help but think that if all retailers were as ethical as this, we could solve more than a smidgen of the world's most pertinent problems.

KÆLDERKOLD

Intimate craft beer utopia

Carrer del Cardenal Casañas, 7 (near Passatge d'Amaden Bagués)
+34 933 024 330 / **kaelderkold.com** / **Open daily**

Tucked away on a little side street just off La Rambla, Kælderkold is a rose among touristy thorns. This bright and jovial space is dominated by a row of 15 taps, from which flow an ever-changing selection of Europe's finest craft beers. Aimed at heavyweight beer connoisseurs, you can choose from pretty much everything from hoppy IPAs and heavy stouts to zingy wheat beers and punchy pilsners. With a Danish owner, it's also a particularly good place to sample the latest and greatest brews from across Scandinavia. If nothing on tap catches your attention, just have a quick peek at the bulging bottle fridges. For something totally different, be sure to sample one of the creative beer cocktails — the "beer mojito" is a personal favorite.

LA CERERÍA

Wholesome, gratifying vegetarian food

Baixanda de Sant Miquel, 3 (near Passatge del Crèdit) / +34 993 018 510
facebook.com/La-Cereria / Closed Monday and Tuesday

Despite the fact that vegetarian dishes in Spain often contain bacon, Barcelona's veggie/vegan scene is surprisingly complete. La Cerería — half musical instrument shop, half restaurant — is one of the places raising the meat-free bar. With its inviting boho setting inside an old candle factory, it's got the show and the go. Run by a cooperative of some seven individuals, the broad menu includes cleansing fruit and veg smoothies, homemade vegan pizzas and wholesome sandwiches. They grind their own kamut, spelt and buckwheat in their on-site stone mill and the aromas wafting from the kitchen are divine. There's also an outstanding selection of teas, as well as homemade cakes and treats that make it a choice spot for a merienda (snack), too.

SOR RITA BAR

Kitsch karaoke

**Carrer de la Mercè, 27 (near Carrer de Marquet) / +34 931 766 266
sorritabar.es / Open daily**

Triumphantly tacky, this quirky backstreet bar is lavished in cheetah
and zebra print, Barbie dolls and collages featuring singers of one-
hit-wonders and Jesus. Thus the scene is set for the weekly karaoke
extravaganza, which sees the glitter ball spin at dizzying speeds every
Thursday night as courageous, alcohol-enhanced performers take to
the mic: the champions here are typically those brave enough to take
on the lamest of songs. Sor Rita is (intentionally) one of those so-bad-it's-
good kind of places; after a drink or two, it'll win you over, and you'll be
hitting the stage for your moment in the karaoke spotlight in no time.

ZOEN

Fine leather goods

Carrer de Sant Domenec del Call, 15 (near Placeta de Manuel Ribé)
+34 933 069 688 / zoen.es / Closed Sunday

When I invest my hard-earned cash in a luxury product, I want to know
exactly where said product came from and who made it. That's why I like
to shop at Zoen, an old-worldly atelier and store. Drop by and you'll
find Rafael Falcon and Lorena Perez cutting, patching and sewing their
sumptuous leather items right before your very eyes. With stunning designs
for both men and women, their purses, wallets, belts and luggage pieces are
not only crafted to look pretty, but also to withstand the rigors of time.
If you're looking for a souvenir that will keep you (and your successors)
smiling for a lifetime, be sure to pay a visit.

cultural immersion

Essential sights and sounds

If it's your first time in Barcelona then there's no doubt you'll want to – and should – see Gaudí's awe-inspiring Modernist creations, the mighty Picasso museum and, my recommendation, **Fundació Joan Miró**, which houses many of the Barcelona-born artist's seminal Surrealist works in a building designed by renowned architect Josep Lluís Sert. But if you'd like to delve deeper into the city's cultural and artistic offerings to dig out the weird and wonderful, try these:

Start with **Devour Barcelona Food Tours**, because as far as I'm concerned, there's no better way to get a feel for a new place than by learning about and eating its cuisine. The folks here work closely with local vendors to create walking and eating tours that give you a taste of Barcelona's internationally flavored gastronomy.

For local arts, **Miscelanea** is a multidisciplinary arts space and gallery, a radical place that shifts and morphs with the rhythm of the city, a place that is unafraid to break the mold and shock its audience, a place to discover the next generation of artists. If this sounds like your kind of thing then you'll also want to visit **Base Elements**, a private art gallery dedicated to the city's most talented urban artists, such as Pez, Zosen Bandido and Peckhamian. Bright prints and spray-paint paragons abound.

Likewise, the **Centre de Cultura Contemporània de Barcelona's** investigative blend of visual arts, literature, philosophy, film, music, performing arts and

BASE ELEMENTS
Carrer del Palau, 6 (near Carrer de la Comtessa
de Sobradiel), +34 932 688 312, baseelements.net
closed Sunday

CENTRE DE CULTURA CONTEMPORÀNIA
DE BARCELONA
Carrer de Montalegre, 5 (near Carrer de
Valldonzella), +34 933 064 100, cccb.org
closed Monday

DEVOUR BARCELONA FOOD TOURS
No address, +34 695 111 832
devourbarcelonafoodtours.com
closed Sunday and Monday

FUNDACIÓ JOAN MIRÓ
Parc de Montjuïc (near Avinguda Miramar)
+34 934 439 470, fmirobcn.org
closed Monday

MISCELANEA
Calle de Guàrdia, 10 (near Carrer de l'Arc del Teatre)
+34 933 179 398, miscelanea.info
closed Monday and Tuesday

MUSEU FREDERIC MARÈS
Plaça Sant Iu, 5 (near Baixada de la Cononja)
+34 932 563 500, museumares.bcn.cat
closed Monday

transmedia will leave you the good kind of dizzy. Past exhibitions have included
a show about housing crises in Medllín and Barcelona, portraits of Mexican
luchadores and 3-D video art from Japan.

For those with a passion for perusing private collections, the **Museu Frederic Marès**
is unmissable. Marès was a sculptor and professor who spent almost all of his money
on growing his private art collection, which consisted of everything from Hispanic
sculpture and polychromed carvings to obsessive amounts of everyday curios.

el born

On the north side of Via Laietana, the ancient streets of El Born date back to the 1200s (when it was originally established as a luxury seaside resort for medieval aristocracy) and has been a mecca for those pursuing the good life ever since. Sophisticated yet artsy, this thriving barrio is home to many of the city's most fashion-forward boutiques, proffering everything from handcrafted jewelry to high-end vintage and prêt-à-porter essentials, as well as numerous museums (including the Picasso). Passeig del Born is the main artery and is graced with countless temples of gastronomy, wine bars and street cafés with breathtaking views of the Gothic Santa Maria del Mar church. If your senses become overloaded, you can always find solace in the neighborhood's 70-acre green lung of Ciutadella Park. Fashionistas, gourmands and expert-wanderers rejoice – heaven awaits.

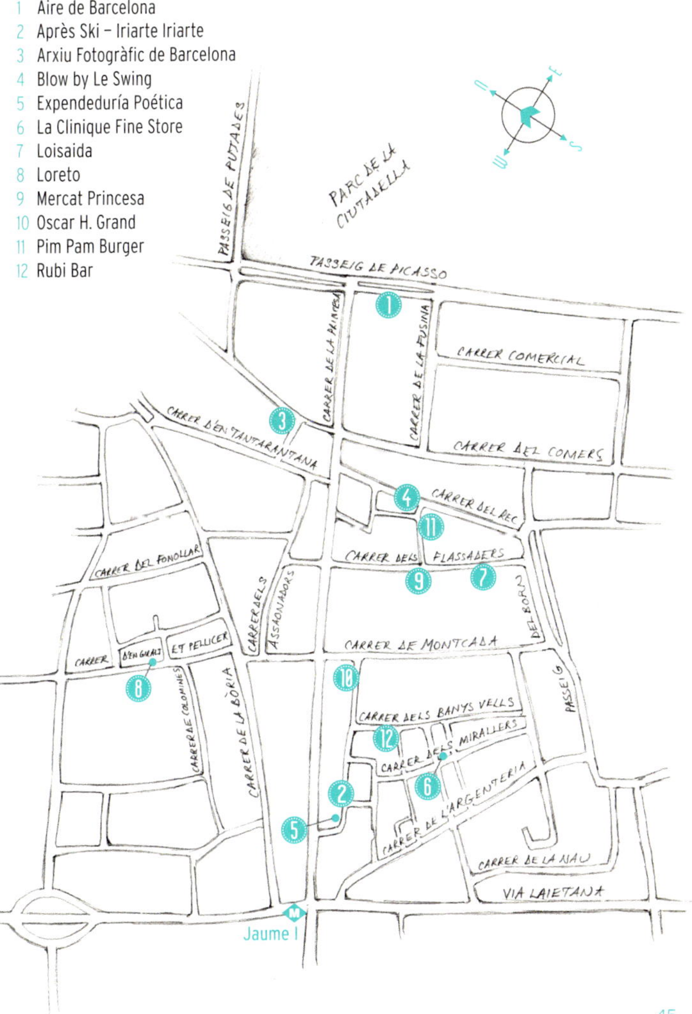

1 Aire de Barcelona
2 Après Ski – Iriarte Iriarte
3 Arxiu Fotogràfic de Barcelona
4 Blow by Le Swing
5 Expendeduría Poética
6 La Clinique Fine Store
7 Loisaida
8 Loreto
9 Mercat Princesa
10 Oscar H. Grand
11 Pim Pam Burger
12 Rubi Bar

PARC DE LA CIUTADELLA
PASSEIG DE PUTXET
PASSEIG DE PICASSO
CARRER DE LA PRINCESA
CARRER DE LA FUSINA
CARRER COMERCIAL
CARRER D'EN TANTARANTANA
CARRER DEL COMERS
CARRER DEL REC
CARRER DELS FLASSADERS
CARRER DEL FONOLLAR
CARRER DELS ASSAONADORS
DEL BORN
CARRER
D'EN GIRALT
ET PELLICER
CARRER DE MONTCADA
CARRER DE COLOMINES
CARRER DE LA BÒRIA
CARRER DELS BANYS VELLS
PASSEIG
CARRER DELS MIRALLERS
CARRER DE L'ARGENTERIA
CARRER DE LA NAU
VIA LAIETANA
Jaume I

AIRE DE BARCELONA

Subterranean spa

**Passeig de Picasso, 22 (near Carrer de la Fusina) / +34 609 338 823
airedebarcelona.com / Open daily**

I moved to Barcelona with the intention of living a simpler life, but it didn't
take long for the real world to catch up with me. I soon found myself chasing
my tail and running around the city to endless meetings. Luckily I discovered
a few places along the way where I could find the solitude I so craved,
if only for an hour or two. Housed beneath the exposed brick vaults of one
of Barcelona's oldest buildings, this underground sanctuary of peace and
tranquility creates the perfect setting to rediscover oneself, with traditional
thermal baths, saunas and an array of health treatments ranging from full
body massages to rejuvenating hot stone and aromatherapy sessions.
The perfect post-fiesta remedy.

APRÈS SKI – IRIARTE IRIARTE

Bags and fanciful accessories made by hand

Carrer dels Cotoners, 12 (near Carrer de l'Esquirol) / +34 933 198 175
iriarteiriarte.com | apresskishop.com / Closed Sunday and Monday

For those with a taste for decadence, it would be a sin to miss this nirvana of women's clothing and accessories. The result of an alliance between luxury bag designer Carolina Iriarte and nature-inspired jewelry artist Lucia Vergara, this is a one-stop shop for locally made souvenirs your female friends and family can really shout about. Lucia creates her jewelry from materials dating from the '40s to the '80s, allowing flora and fauna, geometry and the cosmos to influence her whimsical and often eccentric designs. Carolina handcrafts her satin and goatskin-lined bags in her two local studios using antique tools and vegetable-tanned Spanish leather to create timeless pieces that get only better with age. When shopping here, you know that whatever piece you pick up will boast enlightened design and craftsmanship.

ARXIU FOTOGRÀFIC DE BARCELONA

Transportive images of Catalonia's past

2nd Floor Plaça de Pons i Clerch, 2 (near Carrer del Comerç)
+34 932 563 420 / arxiufotografic.bcn.cat / Open daily

My landlady, Bet, has lived in the same building in Gràcia since the day she was born. I asked her once about the mansion at the end of our road, which, with its looming four-stories and Disney-esque blue spires, looks quite magnificent in contrast to the surrounding glass façades. "When I was a little girl, the area was full of houses like that. Now it's the only one left," she explained. How I would love to travel back to those days, to see the arrival of the first textile millionaires, or the first bricks of Gaudí's otherworldly designs being laid. I might not be time traveling anytime soon, but at least I have access to the two million photos on display at Arxiu Fotogràfic de Barcelona to sate my historical curiosity.

BLOW BY LE SWING

Splurge-worthy haute vintage fashion

Carrer del Rec, 16 (near Carrer de la Fusina) / +34 933 101 449
leswingvintage.com / Open daily

More of an institution than a shop, Blow by Le Swing has been influencing the city's fashion scene since its first day of trade. The emphasis is placed very much on the quality of the stock, with two floors of both secondhand and brand new men's and women's clothing from iconic brands such as Pertegaz, Christian Dior, Hermès and Pucci. The store is also famed for its show-stopping array of upscale Parisian jewelry and selection of sunglasses, bags and shoes. Though the merchandise is impressive, it's the fashion-forward staff that make it such a pleasure to shop here; even the most reserved of fashionistas can achieve a look of timeless sophistication with their help and guidance.

EXPENDEDURÍA POÉTICA

Take-away poetry

Carrer dels Cotoners, 8 (near Carrer de la Princesa) / +34 630 150 903
expendeduriapoetica.com / Open Saturday and Sunday

Expendeduría Poética is one of those offbeat places that creates
a whole new attraction category: poetry shop, art gallery, writing space...
whatever you call it, if you're a lover of the written word, this place will
pull at your heart strings like no other. Fun, quirky and nostalgic, your
experience will unfold roughly as follows: you will choose three words
(in either English or Spanish) from a provided list and pass them to
a poet who will use them to write the first few lines of your poem on a
typewriter. They will then pass it on to a second poet to finish and you
will be asked to pay as much or as little as you deem fit. Tell me that's
not a better souvenir than a Gaudí fridge magnet!

LA CLINIQUE FINE STORE

Retro eyewear, fashion and sundries

Carrer dels Mirallers, 7 (near Carrer del Broslí) / No phone
lacliniquefinestore.com / Closed Sunday

With its chunky wooden display units, minimalist lighting and pistachio-colored accents, this emporium of vintage goods feels more like a billionaire's private residence than a store. When owners Ben and Manu opened their upscale boutique, they did so with the intention of celebrating not only the pieces that they were selling, but also the history and lifestyle that surrounded them. The store is now most known for its unparalleled selection of mid-century eyewear with original, unused glasses from fashion giants such as Vienna Line, Christian Dior, Lacoste and Yves Saint Laurent. Whether you are in search of a huge pair of zany hexagonal frames or need a more traditional pair of timeless aviators, La Clinique Fine Store is sure to dazzle.

LOISAIDA

Throwback threads and music for all

Carrer de Flassaders, 42 (near Carrer de les Mosques)
+34 932 955 492 / loisaidabcn.com / Open daily

Modern dandies and chic quaintrelles rejoice, because this store stocks a superlative selection of both men's and women's clothing, shoes and accessories. Loisaida is by no means your run-of-the-mill secondhand shop: owner Enrique Vivas is as passionate about music as he is about fashion and you'll find the sweetest sounds from the '50s, '60s and '70s here on CD and vinyl, relic turntables and genuine old-school sound systems. There's even home décor and a smattering of mid-century paraphernalia that will transform your home. In fact, a trip to Loisaida (which, by the way, is an enclave of NYC's Lower East Side named after the Spanglish pronunciation of the neighborhood's name) is more an adventurous voyage of discovery than a shopping experience.

LORETO

Handmade jewelry

Carrer d'En Giralt el Pelicer, 14 (near Carrer de Colomines)
+34 935 399 950 / loretoonline.com / **Closed Sunday**

I admire people who aren't afraid to discard the rule book, and must confess to being relentlessly drawn to them and their work. Basque jewelry designer Loreto Velasco is one such person. The intricate, elegant pieces she creates are refreshingly void of blingy diamonds; she blends unconventional materials with semiprecious stones and floral detailing to create her unique ZANTZU range. A sign in the window invites you to have "Breakfast at Loreto's", so pop in for freshly baked pastries and savory treats at their café, before perusing the gorgeous jewelry. As if you needed another excuse to loiter, there's a book swapping shelf where you can stock up on literary goodness, too.

MERCAT PRINCESA

Food hall fit for royalty

Carrer dels Flassaders, 21 (near Carrer del Sabateret)
+34 932 681 518 / mercatprincesa.com / Open daily

This enchanting tapas market is housed in a 14th-century palace with undulating stone arches and a delectable array of 17 specialty eateries. The main emphasis is on tapas and seafood, but you'll also find international dishes such as sushi, dim sum, ceviche, stone-cooked pizzas and beauteous burgers. The central courtyard is drenched in natural sunlight and filled with rows of communal benches where you can chat with locals. The romantic palm-sheltered nooks and snugs offer a fantastic setting for sipping wine and whispering sweet nothings, if you feel so inclined. Stay until late to drink your way through the sumptuous cocktail menu and the irresistible selection of international beers.

OSCAR H. GRAND

Bespoke tailoring

Carrer de la Barra de Ferro, 7 (near Carrer de Montcada)
+34 933 197 662 / oscarhgrand.com / Closed Monday

Prepare to be measured, fitted and styled into shape by Mr Grand and his masterful associates. Yes, I'm talking to you – it's time for made-to-measure tailoring and sumptuous fabrics so slick you'll never want to wear anything else. And don't worry if you're not in town for long enough to get fitted for the full works – tailored suits take between three and eight weeks to perfect – you can still cut a dash in plush shirts, trousers, jackets and raincoats from the prêt-à-porter collection. If, like me, you require a little assistance in the styling department, fret not, for Oscar distinguishes himself by offering first-class personalized customer service, just like they did back in the good ol' days.

PIM PAM BURGER

Damn delicious meat, veggies, cheese and bread

Carrer del Sabateret, 4 (near Carrer del Rec) / +34 933 152 093
pimpamburger.com / Open daily

Conversations (and all-out arguments) about the city's best burgers are rife within my circle of friends. The one joint that never causes friction? The mighty Pim Pam Burger. Something of a burger benchmark, it's what all other purveyors of carnivorous dreams aspire to. Hidden away on one of the many backstreets that entangle the El Born barrio, you'd never know it was a legend just by looking at it. There are no gimmicks here, just a superior selection of beef, pork, veal, chicken and veggie patties served with the freshest market vegetables and serious cheese. The eponymous Pim Pam Burger is classic, the Pim Pam Tres Quesos is topped with a creamy, tangy mix of parmesan, feta and gouda, and the Pim Pam Vegetal, made with eggplant, squash and tofu, means that everyone can happily eat here. Post-fiesta paradise has been found.

RUBI BAR & RESTAURANT

Romantic gin joint

Carrer dels Banys Vells, 6 (near Carrer de Grunyí) / +34 671 441 888
facebook.com/RubiBarRestaurant / Open daily

Rubi Bar is a true jewel of El Born. With its velvet-curtained doorway and flood of incandescent light, it's impossible to ignore. Inside, a narrow space grooves with soul and funktastic afrobeats from the '60s and '70s. Couples perch at the bar with smug grins on their faces, delighting in both the drinks and their company. A dangerously well-priced cocktail menu features all the likely suspects, but it's the gin and tonic (or "gintonic" as the locals call it) selection that really pops my cork. Sample their homemade gins, which are infused with everything from chili to elderflower and vanilla to anise. You'll be feeling smug in no time.

apéritif chic

Where to "do the vermouth"

The greatest time of day is la hora del vermut – vermouth time. Now, I appreciate that vermouth may well evoke images of your grandparents' diamond wedding anniversary, but this old ritual has had a renaissance and is now a Barcelona staple. The concept is simple: meet up with friends before lunch on a nice sunny terrace and have a good old chinwag while enjoying a glass or two. Those six-hour lunches you've heard about? This is how they all start. Follow my lead, hit up these places and prepare to "fer el vermut" (do the vermouth).

Bodega Armando has been doing the vermouth since way before it was considered cool. Time stands still in this tiny space, with old sewing machine tables, creaky bar stools and bleeding wine barrels that fill the air with the sweet smell of the vines. Ask the ever charming owner, Armando, for a glass of vermouth and a bowl of olives, and let the joys of la hora wash over you.

Another fantastic place to sip is **La Bodega del Born**, or just "La Bodega" as the old handwritten sign out front says. It's more of a living fossil than a bar, and Santi, the owner, likes it that way. Despite being just off the touristy Plaça de Santa Maria, its backstreet location and dive bar demeanor means few are rewarded with its stoic charms.

For something a little more cultivated, head to **Bormuth**, which overlooks Plaça Comercial, also in the debonair El Born. Here you'll find low lighting, chunky wooden tables, perfect smiles and locally produced artisanal vermouth that is dangerously quaffable. Don't worry if you can't get a table: my choice spot is actually in the street by the back entrance, where the bar staff serves you through a little window.

Fancy the company of creative types? Head to the foodie haven of Carrer del Parlament, off Poble Sec station. Frankly, all the bars on this road are spectacularly hip, but it's **Bar Calders**, with its cosmopolitan crowd and leafy terrace, that tops my list.

For some homemade goodness, don't miss **Carmelitas** in El Raval, which, despite looking like some kind of East London hipster haunt, is actually an old convent. The house vermouth shimmers with a crimson glow as you hold it up to the sun, and remains seductively sweet and spiced with all sorts of herbaceous heart right to the very last drop. Forgive me, Jesus.

BAR CALDERS
Carrer del Parlament, 25
(near Carrer de Viladomat),+34 933 299 349
facebook.com/Bar-Calders, closed Sunday

BODEGA ARMANDO
Carrer del Bisbe Laguarda, 3 (near Carrer de la Riera Alta), no phone or website, closed Sunday

BORMUTH
Plaça Comercial, 1 (near Carrer de la Fusina)
+34 933 102 186, bormuth.blogspot.com.es
open daily

CARMELITAS
Carrer del Doctor Dou, 1 (near Carrer del Carme)
+34 934 124 684, carmelitasgallery.com
open daily

LA BODEGA DEL BORN
Carrer dels Mirallers, 15 (near Carrer dels Sombrerers), no phone or website, open daily

sant antoni and el poble-sec

sants-monjuïc

Heading out of the city center toward the castle-crowned hills of Montjuïc (home to numerous gardens, museums and Olympic facilities), the shaded streets of Sant Antoni are among the hippest in all of Barcelona. The main artery is the trendy Carrer del Parlament, a street packed with bustling brunch places, tapas bars and traditional bodegas where cosmopolitan crowds gather for vermouth and shoot the breeze. Cross Avinguda del Parallel and you'll find the young, vibrant El Poble-sec barrio, which, despite being home to many of the city's most exclusive restaurants, theaters and museums, retains its distinctly down-to-earth charms. Carrer de Blai is its main draw, a lively strip where penny-pinching revelers hop from bar to bar feasting on Basque-style tapas called pinchos. Combined, Sant Antoni, El Poble-sec and Sants-Montjuïc are must visits, especially for the culinary curious.

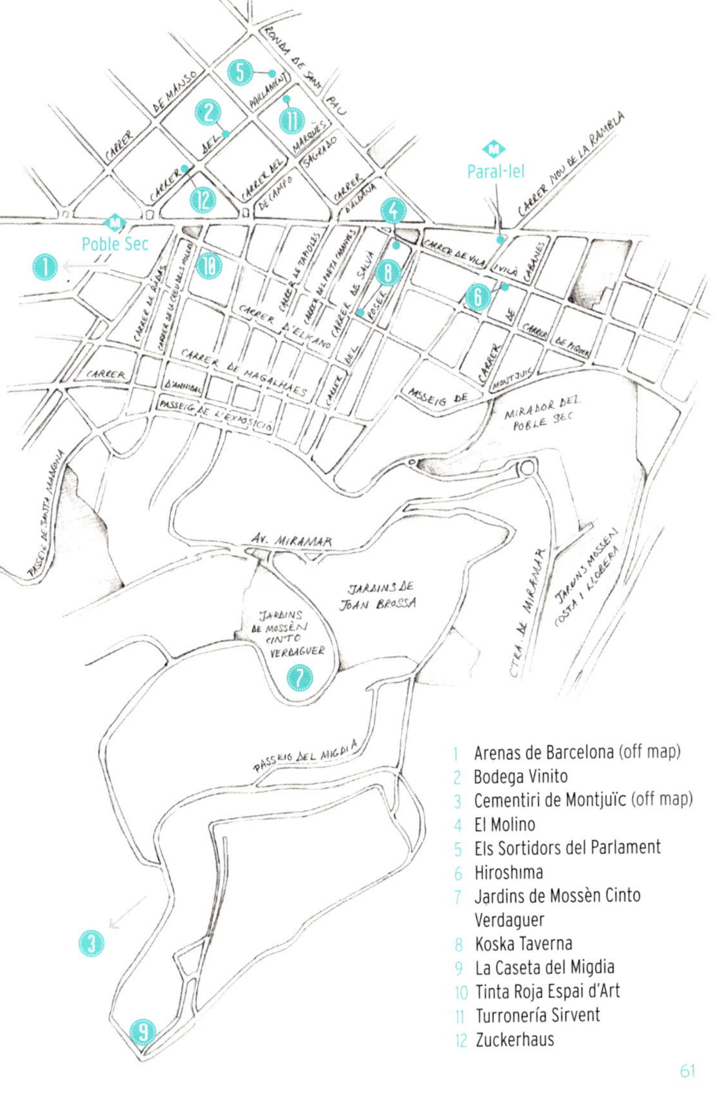

1 Arenas de Barcelona (off map)
2 Bodega Vinito
3 Cementiri de Montjuïc (off map)
4 El Molino
5 Els Sortidors del Parlament
6 Hiroshima
7 Jardins de Mossèn Cinto
Verdaguer
8 Koska Taverna
9 La Caseta del Migdia
10 Tinta Roja Espai d'Art
11 Turronería Sirvent
12 Zuckerhaus

ARENAS DE BARCELONA

Bullring-turned-shopping-center with rooftop delights

Gran Via de Les Corts Catalanes, 373-385 (near Plaça d'Espanya)
+34 932 890 244 / arenasdebarcelona.com / Closed Sunday

Exemplifying their independent and revolutionary spirit, Catalonia banned the ancient Spanish tradition of bullfighting back in 2012. When you see what they did with the city's monumental bullring, you'll understand why fashionistas and bon vivants were as excited about the ban as animal rights activists. In a staggering feat of engineering, the original façade has been kept almost completely intact and elevated off the ground to create space for six orbital floors packed with stores, cinemas and cafés. But that's not why you come here – turn a blind eye to the shops and head directly to the roof, where you can dine al fresco at a multitude of restaurants (I recommend Japanese restaurant Watatsumi, which has excellent sushi), basking in the sweeping 360-degree views of the city, and beyond the iconic Montjuïc.

BODEGA VINITO

Traditional eats and drinks

Carrer del Parlament, 27 (near Passatge de Pere Calders)
+34 934 429 657 / vinitobcn.com / Open daily

Bodega Vinito has been around for donkey's years. Before the area became a magnet for foodies and hipsters, this bodega was a place to come and fill up your wine bottles from the giant barrels. As Sant Antoni boomed, they shuffled the stock up against the wall, stacked the bottles up to the rafters, and added a few poseur tables and stools. The wine barrels remain, which means you can order some of the top local wines (as well as vermouths) by the glass and at very attractive prices. The open-fronted space throngs with a sophisticated crowd and there seems to be a constant turnaround of new faces. Savor vermouth at lunch, wine at dinner. You've got yourself a winner.

CEMENTIRI DE MONTJUÏC

Hilltop cemetery with ocean views

Carrer de la Mare de Déu de Port, 56–58 (near Carrer dels Motors)
+34 934 841 970 / cbsa.cat/cementiri-montjuïc / Open daily

Snaking its way down a hill south of the Olympic Park, this vast, elaborate, quiet cemetery looks like the Banaue Rice Terraces from afar. A pine-scented village for the dead, it's a feat of decadently designed tombs and elegant statues. It was opened in 1883 and has since lain to rest many famous Catalans, including architect Ildefons Cerdà (who designed Eixample) and the founder of FC Barcelona, Joan Gamper. It's also the final resting place of a number of anarchists who were notoriously executed by Franco during the Spanish Civil War, as well as victims of the dictator's brutal post-war revenge attacks. The views over the port and of the Mediterranean Sea are quite dazzling. I can think of worse places to spend eternity.

EL MOLINO

Spectacular cabaret, burlesque and music hall

Carrer de Vila i Vilà, 99 near Carrer de Salvà) / +34 932 055 111
elmolinobcn.com / Open Thursday through Saturday

Avinguda del Parallel is teeming with theaters, but it's El Molino, with its hypnotizing windmill, that has always piqued my curiosity. Dating back to 1898, when this avenue of hedonism was the epicenter of Barcelona's nightlife, it was originally known as the "Petite Moulin Rouge", but Franco's dictatorship and the Spanish Civil War saw it ditch the French connection. Still, the healthy eroticism and risqué burlesque performances continue today, with cabaret shows featuring world-class dancers and the hilarious compere, Merche Mar. Just be careful sitting at the front, as the burly boys' routine sees them pluck members out of the audience for some rather raunchy moves. I got off lightly, but my girlfriend had palpitations for days!

ELS SORTIDORS DEL PARLAMENT

Catalan wine and tapas

Carrer del Parlament, 53 (near Ronda de Sant Pau) / +34 934 411 602
elssortidors.com / Closed Monday

Els Sortidors del Parlament brings a much welcome dose of throwback Spanish sophistication to this increasingly trendy street. Although it's not going to change the world with its traditional pica pica tapas menu, it effortlessly upstages its neighbors with its roguish good looks and seductive selection of local wines. It reminds me of the chic little bars of Madrid's boisterous La Latina barrio, complete with well-heeled regulars and power-tripping business lunchers, many of whom spill out into the street and erupt into frenzied, vino-fueled chatter. Elbow your way inside and order a selection of classic nibbles such as shellfish conserves – a traditional Spanish delicacy – or tortilla with quail eggs and black truffles, smoked sardines and a bottle of red from the Penedès region.

HIROSHIMA

Unconventional theater and emerging artists

Carrer de Vila i Vilà, 67 (near Carrer de Lafont) / +34 933 155 458
hiroshima.cat / Closed Monday and Tuesday

I crave the offbeat and peculiar, and often feel invigorated by experiences that I don't necessarily understand. Hiroshima is a place where I've had many such experiences. Housed in an old elevator factory and run by a small team of experimental artists and performers, this independent arts space will put on anything ranging from theater, performance art, contemporary circus shows, to live music and dance, and encourages critical thinking and reflection. Promoting up-and-coming artists, it is investigative in every sense and offers a totally unique experience that will satiate even the most curious. There's also a really pleasing cocktail bar if you're in need of a little intellectual lubrication.

JARDINS DE MOSSÈN CINTO VERDAGUER

Picnics and lazy strolls

Carrer dels Tarongers (near Carrer Doctor Font Quer)
+34 932 564 160 / jardibotanic.bcn.cat / Closed Sunday

When I first moved to Barcelona, my dear grandfather warned me that I'd miss the greenery of the UK. "It's dry and dusty out there!" he said. One of my biggest regrets is that I never got to show him the vibrant green gardens of Montjuïc, filled with fragrant tropical palms and grassy knolls. If he had seen the fountains of the Jardins de Laribal (next to the Fundació Joan Miró, see pg 42) or the rose-scented Jardins del Teatre Grec, maybe he'd have been happier about my move. But my favorite is the shady Jardins de Mossèn Cinto Verdaguer, which is perfect for a relaxing picnic complete with a bottle of wine.

KOSKA TAVERNA

Most delectable pinchos on famous Carrer de Blai

Carrer de Blai, 8 (near Carrer de Salvà) / +34 931 270 313
koskataverna.com / Closed Monday

El Poble-sec has become synonymous with pinchos, delicious Basque-style tapas that come on toothpicks. Although there are countless streets packed with tantalizing locales, it's Carrer de Blai that is unquestionably king of the pincho route. The objective of a good tapeo is, of course, to visit as many places as possible; but I recommend starting as you mean to go on and setting the bar high with a visit to Koska Taverna. Flavors include stuffed peppers and thick wedges of Spanish tortilla with hunks of bread and cider-spiced chorizo. If you're lucky, there might even be room to feast and gloat on their sunny terrace.

LA CASETA DEL MIGDIA

Hidden place for food, music and sunsets

Mirador del Migdia, s/n (near Carrer del Molí) / **+34 693 992 760**
lacaseta.org / **Hours vary by season**

I set out on my bike one day, intent to explore. After bouncing my way
down a dusty dirt track on Montjuïc, I happened upon a plateau with
a lone brick and terracotta café, where about 20 people sat in the shade.
Children ran free, playing with puppies and throwing pine cones.
Their parents watched on contently, snacking on the café's pancakes,
imbibing cervezas and drinking in the sweeping views of the ships cruising
out into the turquoise horizon. I thought perhaps I'd crashed someone's
private garden party, but it turned out I'd found La Caseta del Migdia,
"Barcelona's most famous secret spot". Go at twilight to watch the sunset
and stay for a BBQ bonanza, live music and dancing.

TINTA ROJA ESPAI D'ART

Live tango, flamenco and poetry

Carrer de la Creu dels Molers, 17 (near Carrer de Blai)
+34 934 433 243 / tintaroja.cat / Open Wednesday through Saturday

My friend David had been hyping this bar up all night. As we entered
Tinta Roja Espai d'Art, he searched my face for a reaction, but I gave
him no reward. "It's very nice," I assured him, "but not quite as wild
as you made out." He smiled smugly. "Follow me!" We ducked through
a narrow doorway cloaked in red velvet curtains and as we stepped
through, were drenched in a wave of glorious amber light. I stood in
astonishment, taking in the boudoir décor, with huge mirrors and
paintings that flickered in the gas-lamp light, and circus ropes and plush
fabrics that rippled from the ceiling. We sank into one of the old sofas
and sipped on classic Argentinean cocktails as we watched the live tango
milonga. David searched my face again. Victory was his.

TURRONERÍA SIRVENT

Spain's finest artisanal turrón

Carrer del Parlament, 56 (near Ronda de Sant Pau)
+34 934 412 720 / turronessirvent.com / Open daily

If you're looking for something *dulce*, indulge in Sirvent's handmade turróns, sweet nougats that Spanish people typically enjoy around Christmas time (though many people – myself included – eat it year-round). Turrón originated in Valencia and there are two types: the hard and crunchy Alicante variety, or the soft and chewy Xixona version. Ingredients include toasted almonds, honey and egg whites, although modern recipes utilize all sorts of pralines, candied fruits, chocolate and liquors. Dating back to 1920, Turronería Sirvent's seriously tempting turróns are widely considered to be the world's finest. Whatever time of year you visit, a few slabs of this will have you feeling festive in no time.

ZUCKERHAUS

Scrumptious confections

Carrer del Parlament, 17 (near Carrer de Viladomat)
+34 677 623 847 / **No website** / **Closed Monday**

Once upon a time there was a salon in El Poble-sec that sat empty for 38 years. Manuela Caruso would walk past it on her way into the city, always stopping to admire the elegant facade. One day the old salon came up for rent and Manuela called immediately. Armed with family recipes, she slowly but surely transformed the place into a magical haven of German cakes and pastries. Between the cutesy decorations customers would bring to her and the sugar-dusted baking tools, it felt as if a gingerbread house had come to life, setting the stage for buttery tray bakes bursting with blueberries and delightfully fluffy cheesecakes. The residents of Barcelona all lived happily ever after, if a few pounds heavier.

BARCELONA AFTER DARK:
late night drinks
Curated cocktails and craft beer
OCAÑA

The days may be action-packed in Barcelona, but the real adventure begins after sundown. There are countless bars and pubs to explore, but here are some tried and tested spots that I consider unmissable.

Situated just a few steps off La Rambla, **Boadas Cocktails** is not only a handy central meeting point, but also the oldest cocktail bar in town. Here, in sophisticated Art Deco seclusion, dicky-bowed barmen with bushy mustaches shake classics to perfection. Order the cocktail of the day and you'll understand why nothing has needed to change here since it opened in 1933.

Many misguided travelers believe sangria is Spain's national drink, but you'll actually find more authentic flavors at **Bobby Gin**. Yes, it's all about gin and tonic here. The mixologists will stir your senses with a huge selection of gins, which they expertly spice up with floral and citric aromas and serve in goblets the size of goldfish bowls.

If, like me, you crave the simple pleasure of a really well-made pint, you'll be pleased to know that the city's craft beer scene is brewing its way to icon status. **Cervecería BierCaB** boasts one of the most comprehensive beer lists in Europe. Bulging bottle fridges and thirty taps offer everything from English stouts and Belgian blonds to local brews and American session ales. The only thing I don't like about it is that there is too much choice. That's why I love **Garage Beer Co.**, which is a short walk around the corner. Owners James and Alberto create their own sensational beer on site, with a more manageable eight taps that emphasize quality over quantity. Don't miss their legendary Riba session lager, which you can easily quaff all night long.

For something a little more bohemian, there's **Ocaña** in the bustling square of Plaça Reial. Paying homage to famous artist and notorious activist José Pérez Ocaña, it somehow manages to attain an air of glamour whilst being wildly offbeat. Creative cocktails and live burlesque performances also contribute to the glitzy vibe.

On the opposite side of the square you can buzz the doorbell of the secretive **Barcelona Pipa Club**, which I genuinely thought was someone's apartment the first time I went. Housed in a residential building, this third-story "apartment bar" is a sort of Sherlock Holmes-themed drinking den, complete with Martini-sipping pool players and the smooth sounds of live jazz. The extra-late night license also makes it a good place to have "one last one" before you mosey your way home.

BARCELONA PIPA CLUB
Carrer de Santa Eulàlia, 21 (near Carrer de Bailèn)
+34 933 024 732, bpipaclub.com
open Friday through Sunday

BOADAS COCKTAILS
Carrer dels Tallers, 1 (at Rambla de Canaletes)
+34 933 189 592, boadascocktails.com, closed Sunday

BOBBY GIN
Carrer de Francisco Giner, 47
(near Carrer del Diluvi), +34 933 681 892, bobbygin.com
open daily

CERVECERÍA BIERCAB
Carrer de Muntaner, 55 (near Carrer del
Consell de Cent), +34 644 689 045, biercab.com
open daily

GARAGE BEER CO.
Carrer del Consell de Cent, 261
(near Carrer d'Aribau), +34 935 285 989
facebook.com/garagebeerco, open daily

OCAÑA
Plaça Reial, 13-15 (near Carrer del Vidre)
+34 936 764 814, ocana.cat, open daily

BARCELONA AFTER DARK:
live music

Where to jam in BCN

I grew up playing guitar and have always been drawn to the expectant atmosphere of a good live music venue. Though I prefer intimate spaces where you can get up close to the musicians, I also love losing myself in a vast, thunderous space and feeling the music thrumming through my bones. Luckily, Barcelona has it all, from tiny bars where local musicians strum acoustic guitars, to big, booming spaces where international bands and DJs transport you to new sonic dimensions.

SALA APOLO

For *tranquilo* midday sessions, there's nowhere better than **Gran Bodega Saltó** in El Poble-sec. Their "vermouth musicals" showcase some of the city's best local artists and provide an ideal setting to enjoy authentic Catalan rumba, which originated in Barcelona and is a happy, upbeat take on Spanish flamenco. Pair with a glass or two of their fantastic vermouth and tapas for the ultimate experience.

When I crave something a little more contemporary and international, I head to **Cara B** in Gràcia. It's an intimate space where members of the audience jump on stage to perform their own songs and stripped back versions of classics, open-mic style. It's a mixed crowd and you can typically expect to see musicians from at least four or five different countries. The bar also stocks an excellent selection of craft beers, hence it's one of my regular haunts.

Just a brisk walk away is **El Cafe Rock&Roll**. Not many people realize that Barcelona is lauded as "the cradle of Spanish blues music". Heavily influenced by swing and rockabilly – yes, slick greasy hairstyles and pinup girl tattoos abound – there's always someone interesting playing here. For similar sounds, but at eardrum-splitting volumes, don't miss **Sala Rocksound**. This gritty venue attracts hordes of long-haired, denim-clad rockers with acts from across the globe. Tap your boots to everything from indie southern rock to country, blues and metal.

Really want to blow those cobwebs away? It's time for the **Sala Apolo** concert hall, which has a retro feel to it with its velvet curtains and gilded balconies. The stage hosts most of the bigger international acts passing through town, but there are also weekly gigs featuring local acts performing every genre under the sun. Whether you're into jazz, ballroom, pop or afrobeat funk, this is the place to get your fix.

CARA B
Carrer del Torrent de les Flors, 36 (near Carrer de Sant Lluís), +34 34 932 225 546
facebook.com/cara.bbarcelona, closed Monday

EL CAFE ROCK&ROLL
Torrent de l'Olla 48 (near Carrer de Tordera)
+34 934 576 097, facebook.com/EL-CAFE-rockroll
closed Sunday

GRAN BODEGO SALTÓ
Carrer de Blesa, 36 (near Carrer d'En Fontrodona)
+34 934 413 709, bodegasalto.net, open daily

SALA APOLO
Carrer Nou de la Rambla, 113 (near Avinguda del Parallel), +34 934 414 001, sala-apolo.com
open daily

SALA ROCKSOUND
Carrer dels Almogàvers, 116 (near Carrer de Pamplona), +34 933 175 411, salarocksound.com
open daily

GRAN BODEGO SALTÓ

eixample

In the 1850s, the government decided it was time
to tear down the ramparts and extend the city.
Catalan engineer Ildefons Cerdà's revolutionary
plans are considered to be among the first examples
of modern urban planning, and everything about
bright and airy Eixample – which literally translates
to "extension" – looks and feels different from
the dark, labyrinthine streets of the old town.
Although Cerdà had socialist ideals, it was the rich
and powerful who moved in, hiring architects such as
Antoni Gaudí and Lluís Domènech i Montaner to build
their elaborate homes, leading to the Modernista
movement and the neighborhood's nickname:
Quadrat d'Or (Golden Square). Today, this wealthy
part of town is speared right down the center by
the glittering Passeig de Gràcia, which houses not
only the famous Illa de la Discòrdia, but also luxury
hotels, exclusive restaurants and designer fashion
boutiques, representing the link between the city's
past and present.

1 Akashi Gallery
2 DelaCrem
3 El Nacional
4 L'appartement
5 Magnolia Antic
6 Monvinic
7 Museu Egipci de Barcelona
8 Restaurant Embat
9 The Avant
10 Zythos Beer

AKASHI GALLERY

Outstanding Japanese restaurant and gallery

Carrer del Rosselló, 197 (near Carrer d'Enric Granados)
+34 931 250 877 / akashigallery.com / Closed Sunday and Monday

Photographers Tina Bagué and Toru Morimoto spent a year traveling across Japan, photographing the country for a documentary. Their lives were indelibly changed by the cultural and natural beauty they discovered and the adventure resulted not only in a breathtaking book, but also in the creation of Akashi Gallery. Inspired by the cafés they fell in love with in Japan, they have blessed Barcelona with their own restaurant/tea house/gallery. The décor is every bit as beautiful as their photographs and the sumptuous sushi and Japanese-inspired tapas dishes are seriously tempting. Don't worry if you're unable to decide what to order, as the set menus are the best antidote for indecisive eaters. Find a seat in the peaceful garden sanctuary and let yourself drift away.

DELACREM

Creamy, natural gelato

Carrer d'Enric Granados, 15-17 (near Carrer del Consell de Cent)
+34 930 042 093 / **delacrem.cat** / **Open daily**

It's the simple things that make life in Barcelona so special, and I firmly believe that meandering aimlessly down Passeig de Gràcia with an ice cream in your hand and the sun on your back should be way up there on your bucket list. There are countless gelaterias throughout the city and you won't go wrong at many, but at DelaCrem, you can be doubly sure of a divine intervention to remember. Owner Massimo Pignato uses fresh fruits, premium quality nuts and artisanal chocolate to handcraft out-of-this-world gelato. Try the pistachio and hazelnut, or freshen up with zesty sorbets. He even has gluten-free and vegan-friendly varieties. The man's an angel!

EL NACIONAL

High-design gastro emporium

**Passeig de Gràcia, 24 Bis (near Gran Via de les Corts Catalanes)
+34 935 185 053 / elnacionalbcn.com / Open daily**

I swore I'd never tell a soul about this regal food hall, but it's just too lovely for me to keep it to myself. Tucked just off Passeig de Gràcia, this sophisticated space is divided into eight distinctly different dining areas, each offering sensational Spanish dishes ranging from nibbles at the bar to five-course banquets at the brasería to an oyster bar. The six million euro investment is evident in its opulent design, and I often find myself mesmerized by the theatrical chandeliers and tropical palms that hang ostentatiously from the vaulted ceilings. With its gilded Art Deco-inspired detailing, it has an air of 1920s New York about it, but the relaxed and informal atmosphere is classic Barcelona.

L'APPARTEMENT

Cutting edge home design

Carrer d'Enric Granados, 44 (near Carrer de Mallorca)
+34 934 522 904 / lappartement.es / Closed Sunday

Most apartments in Eixample are the envy of the housing market: massive open spaces with vaulted ceilings, original Modernista detailing and privileged views of Gaudí's most iconic buildings. And then there's the furniture. I know a few lucky people who live in this neighborhood and almost all of them will tell you they choose to deck out their swanky pads with furnishings from L'appartement. This funky shop and showroom supports up-and-coming designers and curates one of the freshest interior design collections in Europe, ranging from avant-garde lighting and quirky clothes racks to retro kitchen utensils and kicky gardening tools. Their extensive inventory makes it easy to get your digs looking as snazzy as the ones in Eixample. Shame it's not so easy to arrange the views.

MAGNOLIA ANTIC
Unique objects and delicate fashions
Carrer de Provença, 290 (near Passeig de Gràcia) / +34 931 147 203
magnoliaantic.es / Closed Sunday
There's something incredibly poetic about this high-end vintage bazaar.
Descending the steps into Magnolia Antic is like entering an ethereal
cavern of visual and emotional provocation, where delicate fashion
items caress antique stone statues and peculiar objects of desire.
Owner Tatiana Almagro is a true collector, interested not only in gorgeous
pieces, but also in hearing the stories behind them. Blurring the lines
between art and style, you'll find everything from earthy María Antonia
Carrió ceramics and rare Archimede Seguso gold-dusted crystals to antique
medical artifacts and Art Deco jewelry pieces. Pick up a one-of-a-kind
souvenir or consider it a museum visit. Either way you're in for a real treat.

MONVINIC

A magnificent temple of vinology

Carrer de la Diputació, 249 (near Rambla de Catalunya)
+34 932 726 187 / **monvinic.com** / **Closed Sunday**

It's always nice to go home to the UK, but after five days or so, I'm desperate for Barcelona. It's strange, because some of the things I miss most are the same things that wind me up about my adoptive home. I miss the rowdy bars and noisy streets, the constant hum of scooters zipping around. But most of all, I miss the wine. So once I set foot back in BCN, I go straight to Monvinic. Created by a team of renowned sommeliers, the cellar is stacked to the rafters with wines from all four corners of the globe. There's also a creative food menu that follows the changing seasons and is designed to complement the vino. Go for lunch and set off on a voyage of discovery.

MUSEU EGIPCI DE BARCELONA

Egyptophiles, rejoice

Carrer de València, 284 (at Passatge dels Camps Elisis)
+34 934 880 188 / **museuegipci.com** / **Open daily**

I appreciate that the Catalan mountains are a far cry from the great pyramids, but if you have even the slightest germ of an interest in Egyptology, or indeed history in general, you should visit the magnificent Museu Egipci de Barcelona. The first Egyptian museum in Spain, this exhibition space houses almost one thousand artifacts, ranging from ancient jewelry and sarcophagi to hieroglyphics and Ptolemaic-era erotic figurines. And yes, they have real mummies, too. If you're free to visit after hours on a Friday or Saturday, enjoy the dramatic reenactments of Egyptian life. You can also take the Eternal Banquet guided tour and see what Cleopatra ate that purportedly kept her in great shape.

RESTAURANT EMBAT

Modern Catalan cuisine

Carrer de Mallorca, 304 (near Carrer del Bruc) / +34 934 580 855
No website / Closed Sunday

The greatest things in life can be found at the table: a bottle of good plonk, a few close friends and great food. But frankly, you don't even need the close friends to have a memorable time at Restaurant Embat. This bright, modern bistro knocks out attractively priced Mediterranean-inspired dishes. Menus change seasonally to ensure only the freshest produce is used, but you can expect flavors such as scallops with pork brochettes, and duck cannelloni with truffle sauce. If you've been waiting for an opportunity to try the delights of traditional Catalan mar y tierra (surf and turf), wait no more, because their veal and sautéed squid with wild mushrooms is as good as it gets. There's also an excellent selection of local wines, and the homemade chocolate truffles are a delightful ending.

THE AVANT

Women's clothing and goods for the home

Carrer d'Enric Granados, 106 (near Carrer de Còrsega)
+34 933 007 673 / theavant.com / Closed Sunday

Drawing on a cherry-picked selection of quality silk, cotton, alpaca and mohair, local designer Silvia Garcia Presas creates distinctive yet timeless pieces that are so comfortable you could sleep in them. Elegant streetwear, sophisticated evening attire and chunky knits — it's all here. As a master seamstress with a meticulous eye for detail, Presas is known for dyeing her designs in her own color baths, resulting in incredibly bold and vibrant tones. Apart from the outstanding clothing collection, there's also a room out back stocked with equally beautiful home goods that she finds on her jaunts across the globe. From ceramics and cushions to natural cosmetics and jewelry, these objects, both functional and decorative, can transform the mundane to the exotic.

ZYTHOS BEER

Inspired craft beer shop

Calle del Roselló, 185 (near Carrer d'Aribau) / +34 933 485 890
zythosbeerbcn.com / Closed Sunday and Monday

I admire people who follow their hearts and not their heads. Life's awfully
short, after all. Oscar followed his heart. Born in Chile and raised in
Venezuela, he moved to Barcelona to be with his Spanish wife. He did well
here and worked for many years as a business consultant, but he packed
it all in to pursue his passion. Zythos – the Greek word for beer – is not
only the place to taste and purchase global brews, it's the embodiment
of Oscar's dream, and he's not compromising for anyone. "I don't stock
anything and everything," he told me, "I want to offer the best of the best."
Swing by for one of his cheese and beer pairing events, and be sure to ask
him for recommendations on new Catalan cervezas to try.

tapas time

Tapear with the locals

Not all tapas bars are the same. Some are standing-room-only and serve fish nibbles; at others there are generous portions of rustic mountain fare. Some feature pinchos, where you collect toothpicks and are charged accordingly, while others are sit-down affairs where you order from a menu. The crux of it, however, is always the same: spending quality time with family and friends, and sharing plates as you bar-hop.

Head to **Jai-Ca Bar** in Barceloneta for a local, boisterous experience. I visited for breakfast and bumped into my landlord and his amigo; they were washing down their botifara bocadillos with red wine and brandy chasers. *"This* is breakfast!" he said as I pecked away at a croissant. He was also there the next time I passed through, enjoying crispy calamari drizzled in zesty lemon juice, four-inch deep wedges of patatas tortilla and a bottle of Ribera del Duero red.

For a slightly less rowdy time, walk around the corner to **La Cova Fumada**, which is supposedly where Barcelona's famous bombas (spicy potato meatballs) were invented. It's family-run and abuela (grandma) still runs the kitchen, serving up fresh-off-the-boat seafood dishes. There is no menu, but their daily specials won't let you down.

If you want to splurge, check out **Malamén** in El Poble-sec, where Chef David Elfstrand elevates traditional Spanish dishes with Swedish touches: the "simple salad" comes with goji berries, pickled green apple and Cava vinaigrette; the tuna belly, with capers, celery and dill.

Another foodie institution is the ancient **Quimet & Quimet**. Run by the family's fourth generation, this is a standing-room-only temple of tapas, with pickled partridges, anchovies and montaditos (tiny toasted sandwiches) that go down particularly well with a glass or three of their sensational house vermouth.

For exemplary Catalan flavors, don't miss the casual culinary virtuoso that is **Bar del Pla**. Try the mushroom carpaccio with wasabi vinaigrette or the house special squid ink croquettes and you'll see why this unassuming little place is such a hit with the locals.

BAR DEL PLA
Carrer de Montcada, 2 (near Carrer dels Corders)
+34 932 683 003, bardelpla.cat, closed Sunday

JAI-CA BAR
Carrer de Ginebra, 13 (near Carrer de Pizzaro)
+34 932 683 265, barjaica.com, closed Monday

LA COVA FUMADA
Carrer del Baluart, 56 (near Carrer de Sant Carles)
+34 932 214 061, no website, closed Sunday

MALAMÉN
Carrer de Blai, 53 (near Carrer de Blasco de Garay)
+34 932 527 763, malamen.es, closed Monday

QUIMET & QUIMET
Carrer del Poeta Cabanyes, 25 (near Carrer de Blai)
+34 934 423 142, facebook.com/quimetyquimet
closed Sunday

gràcia

sarrià-sant gervasi

Once upon a time, Gràcia was separate from Barcelona. In many ways this barrio still feels like a world unto itself, with its ardently independent spirit and village-like vibe. The lively squares and streets are packed with café terraces, bars, restaurants, and local boutiques and ateliers. If you continue uphill from Gràcia, you'll find the refined enclave of Sarrià-Sant Gervasi, also known as La Zona Alta (uptown). Sheltered from the hustle and bustle, this former medieval village is now home to BCN's rich and glamorous, with modish shops, artisanal eateries and leafy terraces in abundance. It also stages some of the city's most idyllic green spaces – including the mountainous Parc de Collserola, the largest metropolitan park in the world – and handsome architecture, making it the ideal destination for a luxe escape.

1 Babillage (off map)
2 Boo
3 Casablanca
4 Chivuo's
5 Cuervo Cobblerblack Bird
6 GreenLifeStyle
7 Hibernian Books
8 Hisop (off map)
9 La-a
10 Ladyloquita
11 Lukumas
12 Lydia Delgado
13 Passeig de les Aigües (off map)
14 Wagokoro (off map)

BABILLAGE

Magical designs for children

Carrer Major de Sarrià, 78 (near Carrer de l'Hort de la Vila)
+34 934 885 232 / babillage.es / Closed Sunday

I don't have kids just yet, but once Prince Holbrook arrives I know exactly where I'm going to go to bedeck his wing of the casa. Created by passionate designers Marta Capdevila and Noelia Torres, this studio-cum-shop is filled with inspiring pieces of children's furniture, both new and antique, as well as nursery décor and an impressive range of clothing for the stroller set. They also restore furniture, which means it's time to start thinking about which of your favorite pieces you want to bring back to life. It is in every sense a wonderland, a truly special place to start planning your biggest adventure yet. Perhaps parenthood won't be as wearisome as I first thought. Maybe I'll have a little princess, too!

BOO

Sharp men's and women's fashion

Carrer de Bonavista, 2 (near Passeig de Gràcia) / **+34 933 681 458**
boobcn.com / **Closed Sunday**

I've noticed that there are a few shops that always seem to pop up in conversation when I'm shooting the breeze with my more fashion-forward friends. Boo is one of them. The owner, Alex, told me that his goal with Boo was to create a personal space where the fashion savvy could shop for classic labels. The store stocks a range of European brands for both men and women, including La Paz from Portugal, YMC from the UK and Firmamento x BOO, a line made specifically for the store in collaboration with the Barceloneta surfwear brand, and you will find everything from preppy Breton stripes to punk graffiti-designs. Whatever your style, Boo's got you covered.

CASABLANCA

Antiques, art and industrial design

**Carrer de Sèneca, 18 (near Carrer de Minerva) / +34 931 857 854
No website / Closed Sunday**

For insatiable and discerning collectors, the sensual stash of contemporary art and vintage furniture at Casablanca is quite simply irresistible. But it's not only the stock that adds to the store's heavyweight credentials: it's owned by a team of seasoned collectors, namely Meriam Zejli, Natàlia Dualde and art and design gallery owner Miquel Alzueta, who each add a magical sprinkle of *yo no se qué* throughout. Where do they source this stuff, I wonder? Though stock changes hands at dizzying speeds, you will generally find furniture from the early 20th century, including pieces from renowned designers such as Charlotte Perrian and Eero Arnio. Although, it's the anonymous art works that get my creative mind blazing on all cylinders.

CHIVUO'S

Street food and craft beer

Carrer del Torrent de l'Olla, 175 (near Carrer de Santa Àgata)
+34 932 185 134 / chivuos.com / Closed Sunday

At Chivuo's, it's all about brews, burgers and bocadillos. (Bocadillos are sandwiches, by the way, but Chivuo's bocadillos aren't like sandwiches you've ever had before.) Owners Alejandro Bringas and Juan Latuff both came from the world of fine dining but decided they wanted to grow beards and make "food and drink for the working class hero". While the menu is relatively condensed – choose from the tuna melt, barbecue chicken, Philly cheesesteak or the amazing pulled pork – the quality of the raw materials and cooking is astronomically high. Pair your bocadillo with craft beers from Barcelona's finest breweries and, in my book, you've got a top-notch meal.

CUERVO COBBLERBLACK BIRD

Bespoke and prêt-à-porter shoes

Carrer de Sèneca, 2 (near Carrer de la Riera de Sant Miquel)
+34 933 681 381 / cobblerblack.com / Closed Sunday

What's the only thing better than a wardrobe full of shoes?
A wardrobe full of luxury, handmade shoes. Especially if they're from
Cuervo Cobblerblack Bird. This traditional atelier is a quiet and modest
space that transports its visitors back to the days when craftsmen were
celebrated like rock stars. Master shoemakers muse away whilst
you peruse the handsome selection of classic footwear, with buttery
soft materials, timeless designs and precision stitching coming
together to create elegant shoes for both men and women. It really is
a sight to behold and a breath of fresh air in today's mass production
fashion world. Even if you're only window shopping, this is a religious
experience for shoe worshippers.

GREENLIFESTYLE

Modern eco-fashion

Carrer del Torrent de l'Olla, 95 (near Carrer de Maspons)
+34 931 862 010 / greenlifestyle.es / Closed Sunday

I've wanted to save the world for as long as I can remember. I even recall having stickers on my school bag encouraging people to boycott a certain fuel company and wearing hemp clothes that felt like they were made of wire wool. Well, it seems the world of eco-friendly fashion has moved on quite a bit since the days of my teenage angst, which, as Michael Jackson sang, is good news "for you and for me and the entire human race". Owner Carolina handpicks ethical, sustainable and environmentally friendly items from European designers that use sumptuous materials such as alpaca, merino wool and cashmere, all of which are sourced and produced ethically and traded fairly. Shop here and help heal the world.

HIBERNIAN BOOKS

Keep calm and read on

Carrer de Montseny, 17 (near Travessierus de Sant Antoni)
+34 932 174 796 / hibernian-books.com / Closed Sunday

You'd be amazed by things you miss about home when you're away
from it. When I first arrived in Barcelona, I became obsessed with
watching BBC News and found myself listening to the Beatles incessantly.
But what I missed most was spending an afternoon mooching around
a good bookstore. I tried, mind you, but my limited Spanish at the time
meant I lasted all of 10 minutes before I gave up. When a friend told
me about Hibernian Books, I was filled with an overwhelming sense of
relief. It has the largest selection of English language books (most are
secondhand, with a small selection of new books) in the city and, to me
at least, it feels like a refuge: a literary embassy.

HISOP

Edible art

Passatge de Marimon, 9 (near Travessera de Gràcia)
+34 932 413 233 / hisop.com / Closed Sunday

I must have been about 10 years old when my father and I sailed around Turkey and Greece. We'd anchor up and row ashore, rubbing our hands together with excitement as we imagined all the wonderful flavors we would discover. We'd talk to market traders and old men propped up at bars, seeking out the tastiest local eats. Twenty-something years later and I'm still doing the same thing, minus the sailing and rowing. It seems local chef Oriol Ivern-Bondia not only to shares my passion for seeking out the city's finest foods, but is also committed to creating them. Drawing on the region's freshest seasonal ingredients, he creates deeply arousing and outrageously eye-catching Catalan cuisine with a subtle twist.

LA-A

Rustic yet refined plants and objects

Carrer del Torrent de l'Olla, 86 (near Carrer de Siracusa)
+34 932 847 047 / la-a.eu / Closed Sunday

More than a shop, this little emporium of natural and worldly treasures is a Zen space of simplicity and contemplation. French-Catalan owners Marianne and Oliver display their wares around the store as if it were their own home, with pretty pieces of furniture, pottery, candles and various objects of desire that will fit nicely into your carry-on luggage. Though I'd be careful with the cactus plants. Continuing the symbiosis between art and nature, there's a little terrace-cum-vegetable garden out back where you will occasionally happen upon concerts and community events. It would also explain the selection of elegant yet practical gardening tools – new and old – that are available to purchase.

LADYLOQUITA

Local femme fashion

Travessera de Gràcia, 126 (near Carrer de Sant Pere Màrtir)
+34 932 178 292 / ladyloquita.com / Closed Sunday

Small but sensationally formed, Ladyloquita promotes Barcelona-based designers, such as Judith Bel and Paola Sommella, and gives trendsetters the chance to purchase locally made garments without blowing the entire holiday budget. Limited collections include everything from skinny jeans and strappy tops to elegant summer dresses for balmy nights out by the beach. What's more, the retro jewelry, handbags and shoes will also have you questioning what you might possibly be able to abandon to make space in your suitcase. With its elegant setting – the building dates back to 1866 – complete with low-beamed ceilings and colorful ceramic flooring, it's a thoroughbred Gràcia shopping experience.

LUKUMAS

Divine donuts

Carrer del Torrent de l'Olla, 169 (near Carrer de Santa Àgata)
+34 932 182 375 / lukumas.com / Closed Sunday

Where I grew up, donuts came in two varieties: with sugar and jam, or with sugar and no jam. So when I moved to Barcelona and discovered Lukumas's puffs of perfection (lukumakis, which means "donut holes" in Greek) I was distraught with the realization that I had spent my formative years being deprived of such sensational glazed variety. I've vowed that when I have children, I will ensure that such artisanal staples are a part of their lives, as they never were in my own bland excuse of a childhood. Owner and head baker Petros Paschalidis creates everything from classic glazed rings to delicious cream-filled, chocolate-topped and toffee-dipped masterpieces.

LYDIA DELGADO

Timeless women's clothing

Carrer de Sèneca, 28 (near Via Augusta) / **+34 932 181 630**
lydiadelgado.es / **Closed Sunday**

Perhaps it was her early days as a ballerina that helped Lydia Delgado cultivate such finesse and precision in her career as a fashion designer. With her Parisian-chic couture gracing catwalks across Europe for the last two decades, you'd be forgiven for thinking that things couldn't get much better for the lady. Indeed, she seems to have the Midas touch. In truth, she's never been more fortunate than she is right now. Joining forces with her daughter, Miranda Makaroff, whose feminine designs include finely knit sweaters, pleated skirts and sleeveless dresses, this exquisite Gràcia boutique reigns as one of the hottest shops in Europe.

PASSEIG DE LES AIGÜES

Walking, running and cycling with panoramic views of the city

Parking lot on Carrer Manel Arnús (near Passeig de les Aigües)
No phone or website / Open daily

When I moved back to Barcelona for the third time – it's a long story – I was adamant that I would live as close to Parc de Collserola as possible. I dreamed of cycling through the whispering pine trees and picnicking while enjoying sweeping views across the city. I got my way and now live just a short ride away from the trail of Passeig de les Aigües, which hugs the mountains and snakes its way around the park for 10 gorgeous kilometers. Once you get up there, it's a pleasantly flat route, bustling with neon-clad runners and tree-trunk-thighed cyclists. Every time I ride over the dusty, sunbaked soil and breathe in the scents of trickling tree sap, I wonder how I could ever live anywhere else. Perhaps I'll just stay.

WAGOKORO

Refined Japanese cuisine

**Carrer de Regàs, 35 (near Carrer de Laforja) / +34 935 019 340
wagokoro.es / Closed Sunday and Monday**

Eating out in this city can be a rather rambunctious affair at times, though I've come to love the chaos of it. For those times when I require a little more order and serenity, it's a great comfort to know that I can retreat to Wagokoro, a placid Japanese restaurant. Here, you can really focus your senses on the food you're eating without being distracted by dancing waiters and peacocking bar owners. The chefs are master craftsmen and the traditional kaiseki dishes are mini works of art. Order the menú del día for a wallet-friendly lunch, or go all out with the eight-course Wagokoro menu.

wondrous architecture

Eye candy

CASA VICENS
Carrer de les Carolines, 18-24 (near Carrer
d'Aulèstia i Pijoan), no phone, casavicens.org

CMT BUILDING
Carrer de Bolivia, 56 (near Carrer de Badajoz)
no phone or website

ELS ENCANTS VELLS
Carrer de Castillejos, 158 (near Carrer de Casp)
+34 932 463 030, encantsbcn.com

MEDIA-TIC BUILDING
Carrer de Sancho de Ávila, 133 (near Carrer de Roc
Boronat), no phone, 22barcelona.com

SANTA CATERINA MARKET
Avinguda de Francesc Cambo, 16 (near Carrer
de Freixures), +34 932 689 918
mercatsantacaterina.com

TORRE AGBAR
Avinguda Diagonal, 211 (near Carrer de Badajoz)
+34 933 422 000, torreagbar.com

MEDIA-TIC BUILDING

I rose early on my first day in Barcelona, visibly shaking with excitement, ready to get to know my new home. I walked in Gràcia past Casa Batlló and La Pedrera, and roamed La Rambla, darting down random rabbit warrens that led me to Gothic cathedrals and Roman ruins. I eventually landed on the beach, where avant-garde hotels and office buildings line the water's edge. It was on this walk that I fell hook, line and sinker in love with this city and its architectural treasures. When you're in town and itching to see what you can see off the tourist path, I recommend the following.

If your primary focus is on getting to know Gaudí, head to **Casa Vicens**, his first commissioned house. Its Eastern exoticism and opulent Moorish design is void of the curved lines and outlandish detailing that Gaudí later became so famous for, but the experimental playfulness clearly exhibits the beginnings of his groundbreaking seminal works.

To understand why Barcelona is such an important player within the contemporary design sphere, stroll through the streets of El Poblenou. The area's much heralded 22@Barcelona urban transformation project has filled the district with futuristic workspaces. The towerlng **Torre Agbar**, with its flashing multi-colored surface, is the most famous, but I also recommend the **CMT Building**, which looks like a giant metal honeycomb, and the biospheric **Media-TIC Building**, which, with its innovative covering that allows it to automatically cool down or heat up, minimizing its energy consumption, is the stuff of green design dreams.

Nearby, **Els Encants Vells** houses the oldest flea market in Europe. Don't let its age fool you though: the new building is surprisingly modern, featuring a space-age mirrored roof that bounces natural light around and protects the stalls from the elements. It's spectacularly beautiful as well as practical.

Similarly, at **Santa Caterina Market** in El Born, the original façade has been brought back to its former glory with dark-stained carpentry and traditional symmetrical archways. But it's been transformed into a wonderfully singular building by its sinuous, shell-like roof. Propped up on spindly metal legs, it undulates over the entire market and features an explosion of colored ceramics that mirror the vibrancy of the produce below.

la barceloneta

el poblenou

No other neighborhood encapsulates Barcelona's striking contrast of new and old quite like La Barceloneta. The old fishermen's quarter has retained its working-class seaside village vibe while simultaneously becoming a hedonistic utopia of revelry and decadence. The salty backstreets house buzzing market squares, bakeries and the city's finest seafood restaurants and tapas bars, while the glitzy palm-lined beach boardwalk dazzles with five-star hotels and exclusive beachfront supper clubs. To the north, nearby El Poblenou has recently been transformed from a wasteland of derelict warehouses and apartment blocks into a progressive hub for technology, design and media (dubbed the 22@Barcelona district). This seismic shift has attracted creative professionals and the start-up generation, who in turn have attracted a slew of hip restaurants, bars and cafés, all of which are gracefully nuzzled up against the traditional eateries and shops that have lined these stoic streets for centuries.

1 Absenta Bar
2 Balius Bar
3 Baluard Bakery
4 Bar Leo
5 BlackLab Brewhouse & Kitchen
6 Cal Papi
7 Els Tres Porquets (off map)
8 La Malandrina
9 Palo Alto Market
10 Parc del Centre del Poblenou
11 SkylineBCN (off map)

ABSENTA BAR

Bohemian speakeasy

**Carrer de Sant Carles, 36 (near Carrer del Doctor Ginéi Partagàs)
+34 932 213 638 / absentabar.es / Open daily**

Legend has it that in the late 1800s, this ancient bar was where the
city's saltiest sea dogs and wildest artists came to quaff illegal absinthe.
It's seen wars, bombings, anarchy and plunder since then, but has somehow
retained its quirky charms and eccentric crowd. The scene is set with
moody amber lighting, rickety tables and chairs, antique mirrors and
dusty drink cabinets that glow green with homemade bottles of liquid
inspiration. You can still order a glass of absinthe and, if you dare, watch
the bar light up as the bartenders pour long shots into vintage flutes and
set them on fire. If the fire ritual is all too much for you, fear not, for you
can order it without flames, and the cocktail menu is equally potent.

BALIUS BAR

Repurposed pharmacy

Carrer de Pujades, 196 (near Carrer de Marià Aguiló)
+34 933 158 650 / baliusbar.com / Open daily

There's an awful lot of pressure on El Poblenou – BCN'S current cool-kid neighborhood – to be hip. At first glance it can seem a bit underwhelming, especially when compared to some of the city's more aesthetically arresting areas. But when you stumble upon this spot, you'll see what all the fuss is about. Balius was originally a pharmacy chain, and the bar of the same name occupies the former El Poblenou branch. It's a visual feast of moody lighting and gilded detailing that creates a space that's overtly chic, yet cozy. The tapas are particularly special, but it's the classic cocktail selection and locally made artisanal vermouths that steal the show. Come during the weekend for live jazz and live it up.

BALUARD BAKERY

Stellar baked goods

Carrer del Baluard, 38–40 (near Carrer d'Escuder) / +34 932 211 208
baluardbarceloneta.com / Closed Sunday

I was lucky enough to live in Barceloneta for three glorious months in an old fisherman's flat on Carrer de Sal. I'd start my days as the locals did, with a breakfast of botifarra sandwiches and brandy-laced coffee at one of the local bars. Then I'd amble over to Baluard Bakery and pick up a masterfully made warm baguette to take home for my second breakfast – as is the norm here. Led by fourth-generation-baker Anna Bellsolà, the team of flour-dusted artisans here use organic whole-wheat and stone-milled flour to create some 40 different types of bread, from classic baguettes and hefty rye buns to extravagant loaves with olives, nuts, herbs and dried fruits. It's all baked in giant firewood-fueled stone ovens, the smells of which are every bit as heavenly as you might imagine.

BAR LEO

Live flamenco and good times

**Carrer de Sant Carles, 34 (near Carrer d'Alcanar) / +34 932 242 071
facebook.com/pages/Bar-Leo / Open daily**

I was introduced to the wonders of this raucous little bar by a motley crew of theater actors. After squeezing our way through the midday crowd, my new friends spontaneously took to the stage out back to dance along to the flamenco rhythms being slapped out by a dashing young guitarist. The ragtag audience barely raised an eyebrow, and I realized that this kind of behavior is a regular occurrence here: people turn up, drink and, when they feel so moved, dance. But, as I witnessed, when things began to get a little over zealous, Señora Leo needed only to step out from behind the bar and cast one foul glance to regain complete control of her abode. Capricious, free and easy, this is the unabridged version of Barceloneta.

BLACKLAB BREWHOUSE & KITCHEN

Craft beer and Asian-American fusion cuisine

Plaça Pau Vila, 1-5 (near Passeig de Joan de Borbo)
+34 932 218 360 / blacklab.es / Open daily

Within stumbling distance from the main city beaches, BlackLab Brewhouse & Kitchen offers home brews ranging from hoppy IPAs to amber ryes to dark stouts, perfected by their brewmaster in the giant steel vats inside. Out front, there are long rows of picnic tables, typically graced by the presence of Barcelona's attractive people. And as if that wasn't already enough to seduce you, the fusion menu features Asian-American gastro delights ranging from pork belly buns and barbecue ribs to soy-dunked dumplings and ramen with braised oxtail. Oh, and they have live rock music on weekends, too.

CAL PAPI

Rustic seafood and fish tapas

Carrer de l'Atlàntida, 65 (near Carrer de Sant Carles)
+34 932 218 564 / calpapi.com / Closed Monday

Hidden away on an unassuming side street, I've been lured in by the rumble of laughter from jolly diners that spills out of this rowdy restaurant. The walls are adorned with fraying fishing nets, family photos and models of old fishing vessels. Parties of all ages huddle around beer barrels and marble tables, guzzling bottomless glasses of house wine and feasting on generous tapas portions of whatever fish came in fresh that morning. Your order is taken and screamed in the general direction of the kitchen. Moments later, the elderly, magnanimous, ever-smiling chef appears to personally deliver plates of steaming goodness to your table, stopping for a moment as she does so to revel in your reaction with a *"¡Buen provecho!"* before she's gone.

ELS TRES PORQUETS

Enoteca with seasonal Catalan cuisine

Rambla del Poblenou, 165 (near Gran Via de les Corts Catalanes)
+34 933 008 750 / elstresporquets.es / Closed Sunday

Rambla del Poblenou might be the epicenter of the neighborhood's recent hipsterfication, but this little piggy has been satiating the locals with its seasonal market fare since way back when. The atmosphere is relaxed and informal, though things tend to heat up once it's time to choose something from the huge blackboard menus. You can always count on a few porky staples, like melt-in-your-mouth jamón Ibérico and homemade chorizo, but the best way to experience this homey eatery is to enter with an empty stomach and an open mind. While they do stock a heavyweight selection of wines from across Spain, I thoroughly recommend sticking to the Catalan options for a tantalizing taste of the local terroir.

LA MALANDRINA

Steady meat staples

**Carrer de l'Almirall Cervera, 5 (near Carrer de Sant Miquel)
+34 603 621 939 / facebook.com/pages/La-Malandrina / Open daily**

If ever you feel like taking a break from tapas and seafood, or if you just want to eat (really) well without spending a fortune, a trip to La Malandrina is in order. Unquestionably one of my favorite haunts, this little Uruguayan bar and grill is the place for meat feasts and red wine revelry. The menu lists steak with fries or steak with creamed potatoes, and that's the extent of it – but also the charm of it. The vibe is warm, with regular customers bantering with the staff and indulging in bargain-priced bottles of Chilean and Argentinian wines. Completely unpretentious, life is simple here: high-quality raw materials, no-frills cooking and unbelievably low prices. Carnivores, step this way.

PALO ALTO MARKET

Independent street fair

**Carrer dels Pellaires, 30 (at Carrer de Fluvià) / +34 931 59 66 70
paloaltomarket.com / First weekend of every month**

With a hat tip to the repurposed industrial spaces of Shoreditech, London, Palo Alto Market is housed in one of El Poblenou's iconic abandoned factories. A creative space with serious kudos, the collaborative ethos is to invite the city's hippest artists, designers, fashion traders, DJs and food trucks, and celebrate the joys of independent and sustainable trade while, of course, looking impossibly cool at the same time. The crowd tends to be cosmopolitan and it's clear that this is a place to see and be seen. Come and make new friends, treat yourself to something handmade, indulge in gourmet street food and sip on craft beer and artisanal vermouth as the sun sets and turns the sky to candy floss.

PARC DEL CENTRE DEL POBLENOU

Beautifully designed green space

Avinguda Diagonal, 130 (near Carrer del Morrac) / No phone
barcelonaturisme.com/wv3/es/page/525.html / Open daily

One of the first things I noticed when I moved to Barcelona was how
fervently people make use of their neighborhood's social spaces. When I'm
asked why I love this city so much, I always struggle to put it into words,
but it's this inclusive approach to city living that gets me. Designed by
French architect Jean Nouvel, Parc del Centre del Poblenou is a peaceful,
12-acre oasis of avant-garde sculptures, native plants and spiraling flower
tunnels. The ergonomic detailing here is what I think truly captures the
essence of the local way of life, with its elegant seating, bicycle parking,
ping pong tables, pétanque pits, dog walking areas and games for
children. Pack a picnic, take a walk and breathe in deep.

SKYLINEBCN

Sail the Mediterranean Sea

Mooring 2861, Port Olímpic (near Moll de Mestral) / **+34 639 631 149**
skylinebcn.com / **Open daily**

I was completely set on moving to Madrid when a good friend of mine intervened: "Why would you go there when you can go to Barcelona and live on the Mediterranean?" It was a persuasive argument, and I moved here three weeks later with one suitcase and a guitar. I spent as much time as possible at the beach, but as much as I love bobbing up and over the gentle waves that lap the city beaches, it doesn't quite compare with a skippered saunter out to sea. At SkylineBCN, you can choose a sailboat, catamaran, motorboat or yacht, which the team will sail for you through the clear blue-green waters for anywhere between one and eight hours, depending on your preference, as long as there are at least two passengers. City living doesn't get much better than this.

hit the beach

Where to go for salt, sand and sun

In addition to being culturally dynamic, Barcelona also has a four-kilometer stretch of golden sands and Mediterranean waters to play in. Though it's all one long, sandy strip, the area has been divided into several different sections. Depending on where you choose to go, a trip to the beach here can sometimes result in encounters with nudists, athletes and the glitterati. Here's the breakdown:

Starting from the southern end by the sail-shaped W Barcelona is **Sant Sebastià Beach**, where the boardwalk is a hive of activity with surfers running in and out of the water and skaters cruising between the palms. The beach is a designated nudist area, so if that's your thing, it's an interesting place to hang out.

Next up is **Barceloneta Beach**. Due to its proximity to the city center, it's usually a crowded melting pot of cultures where live musicians perform to jet-setters and selfie-taking couples. Hawkers patrol the sands, selling "agua, Coca-Cola, Fanta, cold beer" and "mojitos, mojitos, fresh mojitos!" There are plenty of water sports schools if you feel like getting wild, as well as myriad ice cream parlors, cafés and shops to explore along the boardwalk.

Take a toe-scorching stroll along the sand and you'll arrive at **Nova Icària Beach**, the first beach north of Port Olímpic (look for the golden Frank Gehry-designed fish sculpture), which is a ruckus of professional volleyball players, beer-swigging frisbee throwers and bare-footed footballers. Feel free to join in!

You'll notice a more local feel at less-crowded **Bogatell Beach** (about a 10-minute walk from Llacuna metro station). There's plenty of space to stretch out, cleaner waters for cooling off in and an excellent array of laid-back chiringuito beach bars.

Mar Bella and Nova Mar Bella Beaches are where you'll find me.
I love the chilled-out vibe and spacious, tourist-free sands. It's also one of the most
popular nudist beaches, handy if you want to get rid of those pesky tan lines.

Finally, if you really want a sanctuary of peace and tranquility, go to northern
Llevant Beach. It's far away from the central city beaches and is perfect for
reading and siesta-ing the afternoon away.

All this in one magnificent city. And to think I nearly moved to Madrid!

BARCELONETA BEACH
Passeig Marítim de la Barceloneta, 16
(near Carrer del Gas), +34 932 210 348
barcelonaturisme.com

BOGATELL BEACH
Passeig Marítim del Bogatell
(near Passatge de la Llacuna), +34 932 210 348
barcelonaturisme.com

LLEVANT BEACH
Avinguda Litoral, 114 (near Carrer de Litoral)
+34 932 210 348, barcelonaturisme.com

MAR BELLA AND NOVA MAR BELLA BEACHES
Passeig Marítim de la Mar Bella
(near Carrer de Bac de Roda), +34 932 210 348
barcelonaturisme.com

NOVA ICÀRIA BEACH
Passeig Marítim de la Nova Icària (near Carrer de
L'Arquitecte Sert), +34 932 210 348
barcelonaturisme.com

SANT SEBASTIÀ BEACH
Passeig Marítim de la Barceloneta, 2
(near Carrer de l'Amirall Cervera), +34 932 210 348
barcelonaturisme.com

SANT SEBASTIÀ BEACH

Av. Diagonal
Carrer de Pujades
Selva de Mar
Carrer de la Selva de Mar
Torre Agbar
Media-TIC Building
Glòries
Poble Nou
Carrer de Bilbao
Av. Meridiana
Llacuna
EL POBLENOU
Bogatell
Ronda Litoral
Parc de la Ciutadella
Port Olímpic
Ciutadella | Villa Olímpica
LA BARCELONETA
1 Barceloneta Beach
2 Bogatell Beach
3 Llevant Beach
4 Mar Bella and Nova Mar Bella Beaches
5 Nova Icària Beach
6 Sant Sebastià Beach
Barcelona Metro

BARCELONETA BEACH